TENANT PARTICIPATION IN HOUSING MANAGEMENT

Chartered Institute of Housing
Tenant Participation Advisory Service

April 1994

Acknowledgements

The publishers would like to acknowledge the time and effort in writing this report given by Liz Cairncross, Research Assistant; David Clapham, Assistant Director; and Robina Goodlad, Lecturer in Housing Studies, all at the Centre for Housing Research, University of Glasgow. The report was made possible by a grant from the Joseph Rowntree Memorial Trust to the Centre for Housing Research for a study of tenant participation in council housing.

The work of producing the report was assisted by the comments and suggestions of a Working Party consisting of Irene Bannon of Brent Federation of Tenants' Associations, Mike Elbro of Brighton City Council and currently President of the Institute of Housing, Marianne Hood of the Tenant Participation Advisory Service, Melinda Phillips of Circle 33 Housing Trust, Jeanette Potter of Halton Tenants Federation, Steve Wilcox, Janet Richards of the Chartered Institute of Housing, and Sue Robertshaw formerly with the Institute, now at the Housing Corporation.

Thanks also to May Gunn, Betty Johnstone, Yvonne Shannon and Tilly Wright who typed successive drafts and the final manuscript.

Housing Performance Standards
Tenant Participation in Housing Management

Reprinted with revised forward and address list, 1994

Printed December 1989

ISBN 0901 607347
ISBN 1871 796067

Designed by Edward Pitcher

Typeset by Bookworm Typesetting, Manchester

Printed by RAP Ltd, Rochdale

Chartered Institute of Housing

The Chartered Institute of Housing is the professional organisation for those working in housing. Its purpose is to take a strategic and leading role in encouraging and promoting the provision of good quality, affordable housing for all. The Institute has more than 11,000 members working in local authorities, housing associations and the private sector.

Tenant Participation Advisory Service

The Tenant Participation Advisory Service for England (TPAS) works with tenants, councils and housing associations to develop tenant involvement in housing management.

TPAS is a company run by its members. Membership is open to all tenants' groups, local councils, housing associations and tenants' federations.

CONTENTS

FOREWORD

This Performance Standards Guide was originally published in 1989 and has now been reprinted because of demand. Several important changes have taken place in housing management that are referred to in this Foreword, but the text has *not* been updated to refer to them. Readers are asked to bear this in mind.

Relations with Tenants

Several measures have been introduced which directly affect relations between local authorities and housing associations and their tenants. These include the statutory Performance Reports now issued annually by local authorities and the setting up of an "ombudsman" service for association tenants (in England).

CCT and the Right to Manage

The Leasehold Reform, Housing and Urban Development Act 1993 paved the way for compulsory competitive tendering in housing management, currently due to be introduced from April 1996 onwards. Tenant involvement is provided for in various stages of the process of contracting out. The Act also introduced the "Right to Manage" which would enable tenants to take over housing management contracts.

Housing Management Standards

In 1993 the Institute published its *Housing Management Standards Manual* which for the first time sets out comprehensive standards for the housing service. These include a chapter on tenant involvement and replace the series on Performance Standards described in the Preface to the book.

Mike Elbro
President
Institute of Housing

Marianne Hood
Director
TPAS

HOUSING PERFORMANCE STANDARDS: PREFACE TO THE SERIES

The Housing Act 1988 and the Housing (Scotland) Act 1988 together with the Local Government and Housing Act 1989 are revolutionizing the way in which rented housing in all sectors is provided and managed. Today more than ever before, most landlords are keenly conscious of the need to rethink and reassess their services in the light of the challenges which they face. Some of the most important hallmarks of the new era are:

- more tenant involvement in the process of housing management;
- the injection of a measure of choice, at least for local authority tenants, about who should be their future landlords;
- a pricing of housing services which reflects more closely the actual costs of providing them, supported by decreasing levels of subsidy to landlords, but with housing benefit being available to tenants on very low incomes;
- a system of distributing public resources whether through allocations, grants or subsidies, which penalises perceived inefficiency and lack of economy;
- a more pronounced interest in quality control over housing services by central government as well as the Housing Corporation, Tai Cymru and Scottish Homes;
- increasing disaggregation of the front-line management of housing to smaller units based on estates, blocks or a few streets, with more emphasis upon localised budgets and local accountability.

All of these trends point to the need for landlords to develop and apply indicators which will provide managers with the means of assessing the performance of the various parts of the organisation's service.

Indeed the issue of performance standards is now firmly on the housing agenda as a result of recent initiatives by both the Housing Corporation and the DoE. In June 1989 the Corporation produced *Performance Expectations: Housing Association Guide to Self-monitoring.* Whilst the Local Government and Housing Act 1989 requires that as from 1991/92 local housing authorities in England and Wales must publish certain information about their performance and issue it to tenants and the Secretary of State. The DoE has also stated that it will ensure that similar standards and arrangements apply to housing associations and approved landlords. The DoE is currently consulting relevant organisations about its proposals for a series of key performance indicators relating to the main housing management activities.

Until now there has been very little discussion about what form these indicators should take. For most local authority housing organisations, at least, the most influential work on performance indicators has been done by the Audit Commission. It has devised performance indicators in three categories – **economy, efficiency and effectiveness**.

THE AUDIT COMMISSION'S 3Es

Economy indicators

By economy, the Audit Commission means the purchase or provision of services at the lowest possible cost consistent with a specified quality and quantity.

Thus, in the report on *Managing the Crisis in Council Housing* the Commission suggested that the following were amongst the economy indicators of local authority housing performance.

The number of full-time equivalent staff to:

- manage 1,000 dwellings;
- administer 1,000 waiting list applications;
- administer 5,000 housing benefit applications;
- provide housing advice for 1,000 cases.

Efficiency indicators

The Commission has defined efficiency indicators as **'providing a specified volume and quality of service with the lowest level of resources capable of meeting that specification.'**

Some of the efficiency indicators suggested in *Managing the Crisis in Council Housing* were:

Annual rent as percentage of market valuation
Arrears as percentage of gross debit
Housing benefit administration cost per recipient.

Effectiveness indicators

According to the Audit Commission the definition of effectiveness is **'providing the right services to enable the local authority to implement its policies and objectives.'**

In *Managing the Crisis in Council Housing* effectiveness measures used included:

Average relet periods

Average time spent by a homeless family in bed and breakfast accommodation

Number of central alarm links per 1,000 elderly tenants provided with warden services

Average group or district heating cost per dwelling

In terms of efficiency and effectiveness the relationship can be expressed as follows:

FIGURE 1:
THE RELATIONSHIP BETWEEN EFFICIENCY AND EFFECTIVENESS

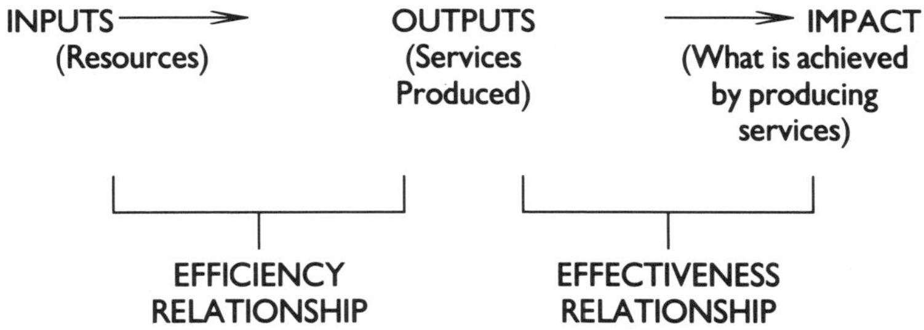

In the Commission's approach, 'benchmarks' were developed for each indicator and indices below or above which individual scores gave cause for concern.

Each indicator was subsequently combined to produce a single Management Performance Index (MPI) used to compare each authority's performance overall, with relevant good practice across the whole range of elements of housing management examined. This approach has been subject to a fair amount of criticism.

Firstly, the selection of performance indicators was of necessity, rather random, probably dictated more by what was easily available than what necessarily formed the most appropriate indication of performance.

Secondly, the Commission's approach, in the view of many professionals, paid insufficient regard to measuring the **quality** of services or the context in which they were provided, as opposed to measuring their economy or efficiency.

Thirdly, the indicators involved such a high level of aggregation of averaged data that while they have some use for comparing the performance of authorities across the board, they are of little use as targets for individual managers in individual situations.

The 'Glasgow' approach

The most recent work on trying to measure economy, efficiency and especially effectiveness in housing management has been that of Duncan Maclennan and his team at the Glasgow University Centre for Housing Research. Like the Audit Commission approach, the emphasis has been upon comparing performance of landlords across the board – in this case housing associations and local authorities – rather than on developing performance indicators for use by individual landlords. The work does however provide a useful improvement on the Audit Commission approach in at least two respects. Firstly, it measures effectiveness largely by reference to the views and perceptions of the receivers of the service themselves; in other words it engages in consumer feedback. Secondly, it points out that economy, efficiency and effectiveness measures do not necessarily all point in the same direction. So, for example although in general terms housing associations were regarded as more effective landlords than local authorities, in that tenant response about them was more positive, they also tended to be less economical than local authorities. In other words individual landlords will have to make judgements about how much more they should spend on a service in order to gain increased consumer satisfaction; alternatively they will need to judge what the sacrifices in effectiveness are likely to be if they were to become more economical.

The research team concluded:

> **'The measurement of effectiveness within organisations requires knowledge of resource costs, the efficiency of inputs and an indication of the quality of service provided. This is best undertaken by individual landlords, not least as they can sensitively monitor the consequences of change in management systems.'**

The Institute's performance standards series

It is in this spirit that this series of housing performance standards guides has been commissioned. The approach taken in these guides is to look at performance indicators from the perspective of the individual organisation – be it local authority, housing association or private landlord, rather than from the perspective of government or the Housing Corporation which might wish to compare average performance between landlords.

Each guide examines a specific aspect of housing management. Isolating performance indicators on individual topics, like voids, allocations, arrears etc. is admittedly artificial, but this is considered necessary in order to do justice to each area of activity. Trying to cover the whole of housing management in a single volume would be very difficult.

The approach is essentially pragmatic rather than intellectually rigorous. Within each topic area we attempt to identify which are the most appropriate indicators against which performance should be judged and look at what this means for the collection of data, the monitoring of activity and the way in which services are delivered.

For most housing managers much of the discussion above is probably quite academic. What they need now are a range of targets, perhaps starting at a quite unsophisticated level, for each element of the service and for different estates or properties within management. This series of guides is written in the hope that housing organisations will begin to develop a conscious approach to setting objectives and targets for themselves which are monitored and adjusted to fit local circumstances and changed in response to customer feedback. For most of the targets outlined in these reports we do not dwell on whether they are economy, efficiency or effectiveness measures, but rather whether they are appropriate local measures through which the manager can assess performance against the policies and procedures which the organisation has set itself.

We believe strongly that the economy, efficiency and effectiveness of housing organisations will be built up from these small beginnings rather than from a system which imposes single uniform targets from outside.

SUMMARY

Chapter One

INTRODUCTION

This report is intended to assist people working in housing organisations to develop tenant participation.

Professional, political and tenant interest has led to a varied pattern of provision for participation.

Three dimensions are present in most attempts to define participation – methods, processes, and outcomes. All should be addressed in relation to whichever purpose a landlord sees participation serving. Five aims are common: community development, better housing management, more choice or power to tenants, greater tenant satisfaction, and helping members make decisions. The skills, attitudes and motivations of those involved can crucially affect the nature of participation.

Chapter Two

LEGAL REQUIREMENTS AND GOOD PRACTICE

Certain minimal legal requirements and powers relating to participation are supplemented by guidance and advice from bodies such as the Institute of Housing and the Priority Estates Project. The Housing Corporation's *Performance Expectations* provides their strongest guidance yet.

The relevant law is set down in five acts:

- Housing Act 1985
- Housing (Scotland) Act 1987
- Housing and Planning Act 1986
- Housing Act 1988
- Housing (Scotland) Act 1988.

These provide tenants (usually *individual* tenants) with some rights to information and consultation and place certain duties on landlords to consult and inform. The only rights that council tenants have to vote on proposals is in relation to Part IV of the Housing Act 1988, known as Tenants' Choice and Part III, the designation of Housing Action Trusts.

In addition, landlords can use their discretionary powers to involve tenants and give them more information than the minimum required under statutory provisions. The power to co-opt tenants as voting members of local authority committees and sub-committees has been abolished in the Local Government and Housing Act 1989.

Chapter Three
THE PATTERN OF PARTICIPATION

Landlords use a variety of methods to contact tenants, divided between written communication and face to face contact. The most common methods of written communication are letters, leaflets, adverts, posters and notices, handbooks and information packs, and newsletters. Face to face contact is made through tenant membership of committees, sub-committees and advisory groups and through discussion meetings. There is evidence that most of these forms of participation are more common than in 1975.

The housing issues which are most frequently the subject of participation include modernisations, estate management, and rent collection. Participation over repairs, allocations and rent levels is much less usual.

Five main geographical levels for participation can be identified: authority or housing association-wide, area/district, neighbourhood, block/estate, and individual house.

Tenants' associations play an important part in many formal arrangements for participation. In other areas, tenants' associations either do not exist, or are not known to housing staff. Levels of financial and other assistance provided to them vary considerably from one authority to another, with larger housing authorities tending to provide most. Few housing associations provide support of this kind.

Chapter Four
THE PROCESS OF PARTICIPATION

Participation can involve a range of possible processes, often overlapping in practice. Eight are distinguished:

- providing information to tenants
- seeking information from tenants
- listening to the unsolicited views of tenants
- consulting tenants
- dialogue, negotiation and bargaining, where tenants are able to influence decisions to varying degrees in a two-way process involving flexibility on both sides

- joint management, involving shared decision-making and responsibility
- choice, from a range of options; and
- control, where tenants have complete power over certain aspects of their housing, and often in practice involving tenant co-operatives.

Each process may involve tenants as individuals or as representatives.

Chapter Five

THE PARTICIPANTS

Officers and members can play the role of communicator in relation to tenant participation, but may lack the appropriate skills. Both can also act as advisers, and some landlords employ specialist staff to advise tenants and other staff in relation to participation. These officers may also play a role in training staff and tenants. Members may also act as enablers, assisting the development of participation. Some, however, resist particular forms of participation.

Tenants' associations can be ascribed many roles, several of which are about communication between tenants and their landlord. Most form to pursue better living conditions, but a social and welfare role seems important too. Attitudes to landlords vary from aggressive to friendly, often reflecting the experience the group has had in pursuing its demands. The majority of tenants (whether members or not) see tenants' associations as useful and effective. Some tenants' associations have virtually no resources such as premises, office facilities, expert advice or training. The wealthiest tend to be supported by the local authority.

Tenants may participate in housing management in a number of different ways:

- as individuals, acting on their own behalf
- as representatives of tenants' associations
- as representatives of tenants in an area, or of the tenants' interests generally.

Chapter Six

OUTCOMES AND ACHIEVEMENTS

Five reasons for supporting tenant participation are commonly put forward by housing managers, councillors and committee members.

Community development can be assisted by means of tenant participation both in relation to individual tenants' skills and knowledge, and in relation to community spirit and collective action through tenants' associations.

Whether tenant participation *improves housing management* is difficult to assess. It seems clear that it is one factor amongst many which may lead to effective performance, and is seen to be an increasingly important factor.

Giving tenants more choice and power is usually served by tenant participation, although landlords disagree about how much choice and power are appropriate.

Increasing tenant satisfaction is more likely to be achieved through high quality service provision rather than tenant participation. Tenant participation is one of many factors, and is seen as most important by tenants in areas which already have some participation.

Finally, *councillors and management committee members* broadly support the idea of tenant participation and see it as helpful, although some dislike particular forms of participation.

So tenant participation is not a panacea but can achieve significant outcomes and is widely supported by those with experience of it.

Chapter Seven
STANDARDS AND PERFORMANCE

It is not easy to devise standards and targets for an activity as complex as tenant participation. Authorities and associations must devise their own in the light of their objectives and resources. Both objective and subjective standards are possible.

Quantity and quality both need to be considered in relation to the methods of participation used. Standards should be set for the issues to be considered, and for the geographical levels at which participation will take place. Qualitative standards, including the views of tenants, are necessary in relation to the processes of participation.

Staff appraisal and staff development programmes should provide targets in relation to tenant participation.

The objectives landlords hold in relation to tenant participation can usually be translated into more specific targets, although some do not lend themselves easily to this treatment.

Monitoring performance can sometimes be carried out easily by reference to files and records. Any existing arrangements for evaluating performance in housing management, such as customer surveys should be extended. No definitive list of key targets is recommended: landlords should select their own.

CHAPTER 1

INTRODUCTION

This report is intended to assist people working in housing organisations to develop their skills in tenant participation, and to help enable them to monitor their performance.

This is a difficult task to achieve because tenant participation is a complex phenomenon, which usually involves a lot more than just the skills of housing workers. Nevertheless the role of housing staff is crucial in facilitating participation. This report thus attempts to provide a guide for action: including the approaches housing staff may take; the skills required; the costs and pitfalls; the ways they may organise themselves and work with others; and the need to set standards and targets, and monitor and evaluate progress.

Using this report

The report is intended to be **used**. Each section is fairly self-contained and can be read without necessarily reading what it precedes or follows. But in a field as wide-ranging, as complex, as unpredictable and as far-reaching in its implications as this, no report can provide an easy to follow set of instructions for perfect participation. The most effective participation is likely to be the product of considerable thought and effort by officers, tenants and policy makers as to the most appropriate forms of participation, the objectives of the participants, the methods or structures for participation, and the appropriate resources, skills and knowledge required. It is unlikely that consensus will always be reached on all these aspects of participation, let alone on the substance of the housing issues involved. Participation is then inevitably fraught with difficulties, controversies, conflict, uncertainty and disappointments. A performance standards report can do no more than point you in the direction of good practice, offer some guidance about monitoring performance and then wish you well.

This report is intended for use by housing association and local authority staff. It provides advice to officers seeking to develop tenant participation in its many different forms; but it does not attempt to provide advice about promoting and developing tenant co-operatives. This specialist and growing area of activity will be the subject of a forthcoming guide by the Institute.

The report refers to the law as it applies in England, Wales and Scotland. Advice on the situation in Northern Ireland can be obtained from the Northern Ireland Tenant Participation Advisory Service.

The growth of tenant participation

Tenant participation has been one of the most commonly advocated ideas in housing management over the last twenty years. During that time housing professionals and policy makers have proclaimed their support for the principle of involving tenants in housing management. Central government has promoted participation through legislation, grants to promotional bodies such as the Tenant Participation Advisory Services, and through advice to local authorities and housing associations. Political parties' manifestos have vied with each other to demonstrate their commitment to the idea. And tenants have campaigned for participation as a right along with more traditional demands such as reasonable rents and better living conditions.

The apparent consensus about participation should not be allowed to obscure the tensions and difficulties inherent in an idea so profoundly revolutionary in its implications for housing management. Participation challenges the traditional roles of landlord, tenant and professional; it exposes private discussions to public scrutiny, and it allows for the possibility that decisions will be different as a result of participation. It recognises that the consumers, as well as the managers, have skills and knowledge to be drawn on. Before looking more closely at what the term 'tenant participation' means, it is worth briefly examining the historical background to its growth.

Professional and government interest in tenant participation stems from the 1950s when, for example, a Central Housing Advisory Committee report (CHAC, 1959) advocated the need for better relationships between local authorities and their tenants. In a 1968 circular on council housing rents, the Ministry of Housing recommended more tenant consultation (Ministry of Housing and Local Government, 1968). Also that year a Private Member's Bill was introduced in Parliament, proposing an advisory committee with tenant representation for each local housing authority. This and similar attempts over the next few years were unsuccessful (Laffin, 1986), but by 1977 Richardson was able to report that tenant participation was established in 'many local authorities', (Richardson, 1977).

The origins of these initiatives are complex, but may include the growth of the scale of government including the post-war expansion in council housing and related concerns about community development in new settlements: the effects of local government reorganisation in the mid-1970s; and the growth of education bringing scepticism about professional and political solutions to urban problems.

'Less than ten years ago the idea of involving council tenants in the management of their own homes had received little attention in housing management circles beyond a few scattered schemes: today it is accepted as established professional practice in many local authorities. Since the early 1970s not only have a number of authorities experimented with different forms of tenant participation schemes, but professional interest has focused on these developments and their implications.'

(Richardson, 1977).

Even so, as Richardson's survey showed, by the mid-1970s only 42 per cent of English housing authorities had any kind of tenant participation scheme. Of these only 11 per cent had formal schemes and over half were in London.

Already in 1975 tenants had been given the opportunity, where local authorities agreed, to take over management responsibilities for their housing in a tenant management co-operative. As the 1970s drew to a close, tenant participation was seen increasingly as part of a wider debate about increasing tenants' rights. There were growing demands from tenants' organisations to have a say in housing management. 'Tenants' charters' were produced by tenants' organisations in several cities including Liverpool and London, and the idea was taken up by the National Tenants' Organisation which was established in 1977. Specific proposals for a tenants' charter including a tenants' committee to advise the housing authority were included in the Housing Bill introduced by the Labour Government in 1979. However, following the election of that year, these proposals were replaced with a more general statutory obligation for housing authorities and housing associations in England and Wales to consult individual tenants on matters of housing management excluding rent levels. In Scotland, tenants' rights to more information, to a written tenancy agreement, and to more freedom in the use of their home were enshrined in the Housing (Scotland) Act 1980.

The Housing and Planning Act 1986 empowered local authorities in England and Wales to devolve management to local bodies, which could include tenant-controlled bodies, and gave tenants new rights to consultation over proposed disposals to private sector landlords. The tenants' choice provisions in the Housing Act 1988 gave local authority tenants a right to be consulted over the choice of an alternative, approved, landlord (see Chapter Two). These most recent changes have altered the balance of power between council tenants and their landlord and thereby provided a catalyst for participation. Councils are now more likely to see tenants as customers who might take their custom elsewhere. Thus participation has become an important part of keeping the customer satisfied.

So it can be seen that tenant participation has been proposed and practised in different ways: some involve tenants individually; others collectively; some are formal and regular, others ad hoc and occasional; some have been promoted by statute and others have developed from local initiatives.

The meaning of tenant participation

Tenant participation can mean different things to different people and sometimes is used to mean different things at different times by the same people. It is important therefore to be clear about the meaning intended at any particular time and in specific circumstances. Here we discuss the variety of meanings possible and their implications.

'A two-way process involving sharing of information and ideas, where tenants are able to influence decisions and take part in what is happening.'

Institute of Housing and TPAS, 1989

'Tenant Participation is defined as:
"the involvement of tenants in decisions which affect their housing."
This definition is quite broad and encompasses a number of different levels of tenant participation.'

Community Development Housing Group, 1986

'... we use the terms consultation and control. Other phrases are trotted out in writings on this subject, such as 'participation' or 'involvement', but it is not always clear what is meant by them.
Control is used ... to refer to the actual structural right to take a decision, and is a stage beyond consultation.'

Mike Bartram, Community Rights Project, 1988

'Clydebank District Council established a sub-committee of councillors, tenants and housing officials to encourage and develop tenant participation. It is interesting to compare what each of these three groups thinks tenant participation means. The councillors defined tenant participation as providing tenants with information about council policy, the majority of staff thought it meant consulting tenants before decisions were made and the tenants saw it as being involved in decisions about housing policy and the provision of the service.'

Platt et al, 1987

Three entirely different dimensions may be present in any attempt at defining tenant participation, and each of these dimensions covers a variety of more specific meanings. The three dimensions concentrate on

- the **structures** or **methods for participation**
- **processes** in which participation takes place
- the **outcomes** or **achievements** from participation

The first of these – **structures or methods** – sometimes receives too much attention to the neglect of the other two. Housing managers understandably want to know whether public meetings, for example, or meetings with tenant activists are a better method of participation. Some structures intended to achieve participation, such as tenants' representatives serving as full members of housing committees, have been the subject of some controversy. Some methods, such as letters consulting individual tenants, have become common practice by housing managers seeking to comply with the 1980 statutory requirements in England and Wales. The various methods and structures through which participation may or may not take place are outlined in the table and described in greater detail in Chapter Three. Broadly they fall into two categories: those involving **written communication** and those involving **face to face contact**.

A great variety of types of written communication can be used, such as letters, advertisements and posters (See Chapter Three). Handbooks, leaflets and information packs have been a popular response to the 1980 legislation, which required more information to be provided for tenants, while newsletters, surveys and audio-visual displays have become more common in recent years. The use of most of these is reviewed in a Scottish Consumer Council report (Goodlad, 1986).

Face to face contact has a personal quality which is lacking from any form of written communication. Sometimes, as at a public meeting, the communication can be relatively impersonal but, informal meetings between officers and tenants' representatives or individual tenants can be enlightening for tenants and officers alike.

METHODS AND STRUCTURES

Written communication — can take various forms of which the most common appear to be:

- letters
- leaflets
- handbooks/information packs
- advertisements
- posters/notices
- newsletters
- questionnaire surveys
- exhibitions

Face to face contact — can involve contact with one tenant, but usually involves greater numbers as at a public meeting, or tenants' representatives, either from a tenants' group or specially selected/elected. Methods include:

- tenant representation on housing/management committee
- tenant representation on sub-committees
- tenant representation on working parties or advisory committees (not part of the decision making apparatus)
- meetings between housing authority/ association representatives and tenants
  - at regular intervals
  - at irregular intervals

The second dimension usually implicit in definitions of tenant participation concentrates on the **processes** or **forms** of participation. Here participation is broken down or unpacked into a number of forms of communication or involvement such as consultation, dialogue and choice. These definitions of participation are outlined in the box, and are considered in greater detail in Chapter Four. It is important to note that these forms of participation – dialogue, consultation, and so on – do not necessarily imply any particular structures or methods of participation, although some, such as control can be associated with particular structures such as co-operatives.

Housing authorities and associations should consider carefully which of these forms of participation are acceptable, or desired, and make clear to tenants if there are any forms of participation which are unlikely to be engaged in. Tenants too may find some forms unacceptable: participation is a two-way process and both parties must understand what the other means by the term.

The third dimension important in defining tenant participation deals with the **outcomes** or **achievements** of participation. Broadly two types of possible outcome can be identified:

- changes to housing policies or how they are implemented, meaning, for example, participation leading to a better quality or speedier repairs service or tenants more readily putting up with the disruption of house modernisation;
- changes to the attitudes, skills and knowledge of the participants arising from the educational value of participation.

Implicit or explicit in some definitions of tenant participation is the belief that whatever takes place is not 'real' participation unless tenants can be seen to have influenced the decisions taken in the direction they wish to go. According to this view it is not sufficient that tenants have taken part – their influence must have been apparent. Alternatively some participants see tenant participation as essentially concerned with fostering a community spirit in an area, or achieving a better understanding by tenants of the difficulties faced by the landlord. What these two views have in common is that participation is being defined in terms of its outcome, rather than the form it takes.

Housing organisations should, therefore, try to develop an approach to participation which recognises the three separate dimensions. It is unwise, for example, to set up a structure of tenant-landlord committees without considering whether these are intended for information giving, consultation, or joint decision making and whether the outcome is intended to include changes to the housing service or better-educated tenants or both. This raises questions about the variety of purposes which participation might serve and the reasons landlords and tenants have for giving it their support.

The purposes of participation

Tenants and landlords who support tenant participation do so for a variety of reasons. Broadly it is seen as serving one or more of five purposes, which it is useful to distinguish from each other.

Community development

Tenant participation plays a part in improving individual tenants' skills and

PROCESSES OR FORMS

Providing information	not a form of participation in itself but an essential prerequisite. Can be proactive or reactive. The written and spoken word are the major media for information provision.
Seeking information	arguably also a prerequisite rather than participation itself. Here the landlord seeks information about facts and opinions, using methods such as surveys, meetings and letters.
Listening	takes place if landlords listen to the views of tenants expressed verbally or in writing, and can take place at a distance and without the tenants knowing their views are being listened to.
Consultation	overlaps with seeking information and listening. The emphasis is on asking for views in order to consider them before reaching decisions, with sufficient time for tenants to formulate their views and landlords to consider them. Face to face contact is not necessary though may be desirable.
Dialogue	involves all the previous forms or processes of participation, but unlike them is likely to involve only tenants' representatives and groups, rather than tenants individually. Most of the common structures intended to achieve dialogue are established for a period of months or years. Dialogue allows for negotiation to take place in relation to specific issues, and implies that both parties have an interest in reaching a mutually satisfactory conclusion. In other words the landlord must want the tenant(s) to accept the outcome and vice versa. This is more likely to be the case where the tenant (or landlord) has some sanction to use against the other in the event of an unsatisfactory conclusion.
Joint management	provides tenants with a decision-taking role along with housing authority/association representatives.
Choice	allows tenants to choose from alternatives agreed by the landlord and can be in an individual or collective capacity.
Control	*not* the only 'real' form of participation, and arguably not a form of 'taking part' at all in that tenants are enabled to take over and directly run certain aspects of their housing services (within the law).

capacities which in turn leads to a stronger sense of community and to a reduction in social problems. Tenants are enabled to play a greater part in determining the future of their area and to be more effective participants. Tenant participation is thus seen as a valuable activity in its own right.

Better housing management

Tenant participation assists better decision making by providing information which can be taken into account in service delivery and planning. This can lead to better decisions and more satisfied tenants. Participation is, therefore, a means to an end.

More choice or power to tenants

Participation can be seen as essentially bound up with the moral right of tenants to influence their own living conditions, either on the basis that the tenant pays or because of an implicit view about the nature of a democratic society.

Tenant satisfaction

Participation plays an important part in effective housing management, in which effectiveness is strongly associated with tenant satisfaction. Participation is, therefore, a means to the end of achieving more satisfied tenants.

Helping councillors or committee members

Tenant participation can be seen as directly in conflict with the roles of councillors and committee members, but an increasingly common view, is that the participation of tenants can complement and supplement the role of policy makers. Tenants are seen as providing useful information to committee members who can assist the tenants to present their point of view especially when something appears to have gone wrong with the system for handling complaints. Tenant participation can, therefore, assist policy makers to be more effective.

The participants

Tenant participation potentially involves three principal sets of participants: tenants, housing officers, and lay members of the authority or association. Tenants include individual tenants and tenants' groups. Others who may become involved include tenants' advisers, MPs, community workers, and officials from a variety of departments and agencies.

The attitudes, skills and motivations of each of these groups can have a crucial effect on the nature of the participation that takes place, and on the outcome or achievements. These issues are considered in greater detail in Chapter Five.

ferences

Bartram Mike (1988) *Consulting Tenants – Council Initiatives in the Late 1980s*, Community Rights Project, London

Central Housing Advisory Committee (1959) *Councils and their Houses*, HMSO, London

Community Development Housing Group (1986) *But Will it Fly, Mr. Wright?* TPAS, Glasgow

Goodlad Robina (1986) *Telling the Tenants*, Scottish Consumer Council, Glasgow

Institute of Housing and Tenant Participation Advisory Service (1989) In a letter to the authors

Laffin Martin (1986) *Professionalism and Policy: The Role of the Professions in the Central – Local Government Relationship*, Avebury, Aldershot

Ministry of Housing and Local Government (1968) *Increases in Rents of Local Authority Housing: Prices and Incomes Act 1968, Sections 10–12*, Circular 37/68, MHLG, London

Platt Steve, Piepe Rita and Smyth Judith (1987) *Heard or Ignored*, NFHA, London

Richardson Ann (1977) *Tenant Participation in Council Housing Management*, Housing Development Directorate, DoE, London

CHAPTER 2

LEGAL REQUIREMENTS AND GOOD PRACTICE

This chapter describes the legal provisions and guidance available to housing authorities and associations in relation to tenant participation. The legal requirements are fairly minimal and have been supplemented in recent years by advice, guidance and recommendations, particularly for housing associations registered with the Housing Corporation. This chapter therefore summarises for housing authorities and associations what they must *do, what they* can *do, and what they are* advised *to do in order to comply with the letter and spirit of the statutory provisions for tenant participation.*

The law

Broadly the law provides tenants with some rights and landlords with some duties, but these are generally restricted to the provision of information, and consultation with individual tenants rather than with tenants collectively. In addition authorities and associations can use their discretionary powers to inform, consult or involve tenants in ways that go beyond what is required by law. This can involve tenants' representatives in dialogue or other forms of contact with the staff or members of the authority or association. The principal statutes which define the duties and rights of landlords and tenants are:

- Housing Act 1985
- Housing (Scotland) Act 1987
- Housing and Planning Act 1986
- Housing Act 1988
- Housing (Scotland) Act 1988.

ousing Act 1985

Sections 104 and 105 require authorities and associations in England and Wales to inform and consult secure tenants about particular matters.

Section 104 places a duty on authorities and associations to publish and provide all their secure tenants with a copy of information 'explaining in simple terms' (a) the 'express terms' of their secure tenancies, (b) the provisions of Parts IV and V of the Act (tenants' rights), and (c) the provisions of Sections 11 to 16 of the Landlord and Tenant Act 1985 (that is, the landlord's repairing obligations). This includes informing tenants about the arrangements which exist for consultation, and for applicants to inspect the information they provided in their application.

Section 105 requires authorities and associations to maintain such arrangements as **they** consider appropriate for informing secure tenants about any proposals for changes in matters of housing management which will affect them substantially, so as to enable tenants to make their views known, and to consider these before making any decisions. Housing management matters are defined as management, maintenance, improvement, demolition and the provision of services or amenities. Rent levels and service charges are specifically excluded. Landlords are obliged to publish these arrangements: housing associations must send copies to the Housing Corporation and to all local authorities in whose areas they let housing, while local authorities must make copies available for inspection at no charge or for purchase at a 'reasonable' charge.

Section 106 requires authorities and associations to publish and/or make available their rules and procedures for the allocation of their housing and have arrangements which enable applicants to inspect the information they provide in their applications.

These provisions apply also to New Town Development Corporations. They do not apply to assured tenancies provided by associations under the Housing Act 1988, but associations are expected to comply with the requirements of the Tenants' Guarantee published by the Housing Corporation for assured tenancies and which broadly replicates the statutory rights of secure tenants to information and consultation (Housing Corporation, 1988, 1989).

Housing (Scotland) Act 1987

Sections 21, 53 and 54 require authorities and associations in Scotland to inform secure tenants about particular matters, and reach agreement about tenancy conditions.

Section 21 requires authorities and associations to publish and make available their rules and procedures for the allocation of their housing, and to have arrangements which enable applicants to inspect any information provided by them in their application.

Section 53 requires authorities and associations to draw up a written lease for secure tenants. Section 54 gives tenants and landlords the right to approach the Sheriff Court over failures to agree changes.

These provisions apply also to tenants of New Town Development Corporations and Scottish Homes, but not to assured tenancies offered by housing associations under the Housing (Scotland) Act 1988. However, the Scottish Federation of Housing Associations has produced a model tenancy agreement which broadly replicates the statutory rights of secure tenants to information, and which the Federation hopes its member housing associations will adopt.

Housing and Planning Act 1986

Section 6 amended the 1985 Housing Act to give secure tenants rights to consultation over the housing authority's proposals to dispose of their homes to a private landlord. Schedule 1 added Schedule 3A to the 1985 Act. These provisions require housing authorities which are considering such a disposal to a private sector landlord to 'serve notice in writing on the tenant informing him' (sic) of details of the proposal including the identity of the potential new landlord, the 'likely consequences for the tenant', and of the rights to buy which would continue to exist. A ballot is not required in law. The authority must consider any representations received, and the Secretary of State will withhold consent if he or she believes a majority do not 'wish the disposal to proceed'. Individual tenants cannot opt out of any transfer that results.

Sections 10 and 11 replace Section 27 of the Housing Act 1985 and provide that in certain circumstances a tenants' association may compel a housing authority to take into consideration a proposal to establish a management or ownership co-operative. Authorities are required to state reasons for not accepting such a proposal. A tenants' association must have at least half its members living in the houses affected, and at least half the tenants of the houses must be members of the association. There must be at least 50 members who live in the area or alternatively the association must be registered under the Industrial and Provident Societies Act 1965.

Section 10 enables housing authorities to enter into a management agreement with another body. The housing authority must inform tenants in writing of any such proposal. The terms of the agreement and the identity of the manager must be approved by the Secretary of State, who will not give approval unless a majority of tenants are in favour.

ousing Act 1988

This Act has indirectly provided local authorities with a strong incentive to develop tenant participation, while not extending the rights of council tenants as such to participation. The prospect that alternative landlords might attract tenants away from the council sector has meant that councils increasingly look to tenant participation as a means of ensuring tenant satisfaction.

The Housing Act 1988 reforms the Rent Acts and the relationship between private sector (including housing assocation) landlords and tenants; provides for the establishment of housing action trusts; gives rights to approved landlords to acquire houses occupied by secure tenants; and establishes important differences between the rights of secure (council and new town) tenants and assured (housing association and private) tenants. Provision for tenant consultation is contained in Section 61 (housing action trusts) and in Sections 102, 103 and 105 (transfers of stock under the tenants' choice arrangements). These rights to consultation over disposals and transfers of ownership, however, are of a different order from the rights to consultation on management described above.

Assured tenants have no rights to consultation over housing management matters, but the Housing Corporation has made clear in advice to housing associations (1988, 1989) that they are expected to inform and consult tenants, and that provision for this should be included in tenancy agreements. In addition the National Federation of Housing Associations (NFHA) has produced a model tenancy agreement which includes provision for consultation, and which the Federation hopes its member housing associations will adopt.

Section 61 provides that where a housing action trust (HAT) is proposed, tenants must be consulted. The Secretary of State has to inform the tenants, and arrange or conduct 'a ballot or poll' 'to establish their opinions'. In the event of a majority vote against the proposals, the Secretary of State will not permit the HAT to proceed.

Sections 102 and 103 set down the outline procedure for a ballot, carried out by an independent teller, of tenants affected by a tenants' choice proposal from a potential new landlord. Regulations govern the way the consultation should be carried out. The application can proceed, provided that 50 per cent or more of those entitled to vote have voted; *and* less than 50 per cent of the tenants entitled to vote have voted to stay with their present landlord.

These provisions allow for the possibility that the potential new landlord can be the tenants themselves, organised as a co-operative, trust or other body.

Section 105 deals with subsequent disposals of former council housing. The prospective landlord (who cannot be a local authority), must consult the tenants affected and the Secretary of State is compelled to 'have regard' to the views expressed, but is not required to accept them.

Section 135 and Schedule 16 clarify the right of tenants in Scotland to be consulted about the authority's proposals to dispose of their housing which would be likely to result in them ceasing to be secure tenants. It adds Section 87B, and Schedule 6A to the Housing (Scotland) Act 1987, which sets out the procedure for consultation. The provisions are equivalent to those described above for England and Wales in the Housing and Planning Act 1986.

Housing (Scotland) Act 1988

This Act provides broadly equivalent legislation for Scotland to the Housing Act 1988 though with some important differences affecting tenants' choice. Section 58 provides individual council tenants with the right to agree to or prevent their house being acquired by a prospective new landlord. This provision also applies to New Town Development Corporation and Scottish Homes tenants.

Discretionary powers

Both local authorities and housing associations have the capacity to involve tenants on their formal decision-making committees or less formally on advisory or consultative groups, providing this is done within the law (for local authorities) or within the rules of associations.

The Local Government Act 1972 and the Local Government (Scotland) Act 1973 defined the limits to formal involvement by co-opted members on housing or other committees. The Local Government and Housing Act 1989 amends these provisions to prevent co-opted members of housing committees or sub-committees from voting. This means that tenant co-optees must serve only in an advisory capacity. However, they retain their rights to vote on advisory committees.

Advice and guidance to landlords

Since the 1970s central government has, through circulars and other means, encouraged local authorities to develop tenant participation. Circulars include *SDD Circular 14/77: Tenant Participation and Housing Co-operatives*, which encouraged Scottish local authorities to take advantage of 1975 legislation which allowed for the establishment of tenant management co-operatives. Other forms of participation were encouraged but given little elaboration. In 1977, the DoE provided information about *Tenant Participation in Council Housing Management* in an occasional paper (Richardson, 1977) and in the same year issued *Getting Tenants Involved*, a handbook on methods of tenant participation.

Housing associations too have been encouraged both by the Housing Corporation and by the NFHA to consider public accountability and tenant participation. In 1989 the Corporation issued *Performance Expectations* providing their strongest guidance yet on ways in which associations are expected to demonstrate their accountability to tenants and prospective tenants as well as to the Corporation. Housing Corporation Circulars 3/78 and 11/80 are also relevant, as is the NFHA's *Standards for Housing Management* (1987). Useful, though out of print, are two earlier NFHA guides to aspects of the Housing Act 1980 – *Tenants' Information* and *Tenant Consultation*.

Central government has also encouraged tenant participation by assisting the funding of Tenant Participation Advisory Services in all four parts of the United Kingdom. Their publications and other work provide advice both to landlords and tenants. Also assisted by central government, as well as individual local authorities, has been the work of the Priority Estates Project in England and Wales, which has consistently seen tenant involvement as an essential feature of improving run-down council estates.

Other bodies such as the Institute of Housing and the local authority associations have promoted tenant participation with advice to local authorities and housing associations. In addition, tenants' organisations have consistently argued for tenant involvement and provided landlords with advice about how they think it can best take place.

'There is no model that can be applied to all or even a range of similar circumstances, and we have referred to examples of "good practice" relating to different aspects of this right (to consultation). Opinion is also divided amongst tenants as to which models of consultation to adopt. Nevertheless, we consider that, irrespective of the actual methods of consultation adopted, all authorities should provide their tenants with clear guidelines and commitments on: what matters will be subject to consultation; who will be involved; how the process of consultation fits in with the council's own decision making processes and how tenants' views will be taken into account. Unless more authorities commit themselves on these points, it is difficult to envisage this right having much effect.'

Kay et al, undated

'We believe that it is very important that tenants be involved in the management of their homes. If this is not permitted and encouraged, a valuable resource is being wasted, and the risk of providing unsuitable services is increased.'

NFHA, 1985

'Local authorities are keen to involve tenants in decisions about their homes and environments . . . (and) are increasingly eager to disprove the old idea of housing departments as unresponsive and bureaucratic. Often when pointing to particular examples of good practice councils emphasise the important role that tenant involvement played in making the scheme a success.'

Association of Metropolitan Authorities, 1986

'It is essential that landlords work with residents and their organised representatives in whatever way they can. This takes time and a significant input from local staff.'

Anne Power, 1987a

'Consultation with residents on a PEP estate is needed early in the project's development.

. . . Tenants associations where they exist, will want to have a say in the development of the project and help organise the consultation.

Resident representatives are necessary for any effective ongoing liaison between the Council and the Community.

It is important to ensure that racial minorities on multi-racial estates are represented.'

Anne Power, 1987b

'A central objective of all associations must be to provide, as far as possible, services that tenants and licensees need and want, and in ways which are most convenient to them. To achieve this, associations have to be clear about three things: the general areas in which it is proper for tenants' and licensees' views to have influence: the best methods of obtaining these views in different circumstances; and how to ensure that they are given proper attention. The three main means of achieving this objective are: obtaining feedback on existing services and activities; consulting on proposals for change; and formal participation in the decision making of the association.'

NFHA, 1987

'We believe that there has to be a fundamental change in the balance of control between local authorities and their tenants in how council housing is run. All councils need to establish the means for involving tenants in decision making on their properties at the individual, estate and borough wide level. Those councils who have done nothing to promote and encourage the formation of tenants' associations on their estates must do so. Those councils who are hostile to the tenants' movement have no right to be landlords.'

Institute of Housing, 1987

'An underlying objective of any housing association must be to provide the highest possible service to its consumers, i.e. tenants and prospective tenants.

Associations should be answerable to tenants and should find ways of encouraging and enabling tenants to influence policy and practice . . .

ASSOCIATIONS ARE EXPECTED TO:

6.1 Grant tenancies on terms which comply with the law and the Tenants' Guarantee . . .

6.6 Provide effective services, including estate management services, taking account of tenants' need and wishes.

6.7 Consult with tenants and obtain their feedback in effective and structured ways.

6.8 Be readily accessible to their tenants for information, advice and services.'

Housing Corporation, 1989

References

Association of Metropolitan Authorities (1986) *Achievements in Council Housing*, AMA, London

Department of the Environment (1977) *Getting Tenants Involved*, DoE, London

Housing Corporation (1978) *In the Public Eye*, Circular HC3/78, The Housing Corporation, London

Housing Corporation (1980) *The Housing Corporation and Housing Associations*, Circular HC11/80, The Housing Corporation, London

Housing Corporation (1988) *The Tenants' Guarantee: Guidance on Housing Management Practice for Assured Tenancies*, Circular HC43/88, The Housing Corporation, London

References

Housing Corporation (1989) *Performance Expectations: Housing Association Guide to Self-monitoring,* The Housing Corporation, London

Institute of Housing (1987) *Preparing for Change – Public Sector Housing: Future, Use, Control and Management*, Report by a working party, Institute of Housing, London

Kay Adah, Legg Charles and Foot Jane. (undated) *The 1980 Tenants' Rights in Practice*, The City University, London

NFHA (1980) *Tenant Consultation*, NFHA, London

NFHA (1980) *Tenants' Information*, NFHA, London

NFHA (1985) *Report of the Inquiry into British Housing* chaired by HRH The Duke of Edinburgh, NFHA, London

NFHA (1987) *Standards for Housing Management*, London

Power Anne (1987a) *The Guide to Local Housing Management No. 1: The PEP Model,* DoE/Welsh Office, London/Cardiff

Power Anne (1987b) *The PEP Guide to Local Housing Management No. 3: Guidelines for Setting up New Projects*, DoE/Welsh Office, London/Cardiff

THE PATTERN OF PARTICIPATION

3

CHAPTER

This chapter looks at the methods that landlords use to involve their tenants; at the issues dealt with at a variety of geographical levels; and at the role of tenants' associations and the resources available to them. The chapter is based largely on surveys carried out by Glasgow University into arrangements for tenant participation by local authorities in England, Scotland and Wales and of housing associations in England; on six local authority case studies; and on the findings of the research reports published by the NFHA on tenant involvement in housing associations (Crook, 1985; Platt et al, 1987).

The focus here is on the extent, structures and methods of tenant participation. Information about the quality and nature of the participation is considered in later chapters. Methods of participation between landlord and tenant are divided between those involving **written communication** and those where there is **face to face contact**.

The local authority results represent responses from 282 (62 per cent) councils in Britain, and refer to the years 1986 or 1987. The results are referred to as 'national LA survey' in the tables that follow. It is likely that since then, the picture has changed and arrangements for tenant participation have increased, partly as a result of the reaction to the 1988 Housing Acts. The survey of housing associations with a stock of 200 or more properties, carried out over the same period, covers 77 associations in England (39 per cent of such associations). The results are referred to as 'HA survey' below. The HA survey and part of the national LA survey were funded by the Department of the Environment (Centre for Housing Research, 1989). The information from housing associations relates to those whose main activity is the provision of general needs housing. The survey of tenants' associations was completed in six local authority case study areas in 1988. Responses came from 142 tenants' associations in five of the areas. The research was funded by the Joseph Rowntree Memorial Trust.

The local authority results represent responses from 282 (62 per cent) councils in Britain, and refer to the years 1986 or 1987. The results are referred to as 'national LA survey' in the tables that follow. It is likely that since then, the picture has changed and arrangements for tenant participation have increased, partly as a result of the reaction to the 1988 Housing Acts. The survey of housing associations with a stock of 200 or more properties, carried out over the same period, covers 77 associations in England (39 per cent of such associations). The results are referred to as 'HA survey' below. The HA survey and part of the national LA survey were funded by the Department of the Environment (Centre for Housing Research, 1989). The information from housing associations relates to those whose main activity is the provision of general needs housing. The survey of tenants' associations was completed in six local authority case study areas in 1988. Responses came from 142 tenants' associations in five of the areas. The research was funded by the Joseph Rowntree Memorial Trust.

The written word

At the most basic level of participation, local authority and housing association landlords communicate in writing with their tenants either individually or through tenants' groups.

The main methods of written communication with tenants are:

- letters
- leaflets
- adverts, posters and notices
- handbooks and information packs
- newsletters.

Other methods such as display boards and questionnaires are also sometimes used.

Different methods may fulfil one or several roles. Some may be more

TABLE 1

Written communications to council tenants: proportions of authorities using different methods

	London Boroughs %	Met. Districts %	English Non-Met. Districts %	Welsh Districts %	Scottish Districts %	Total %
etters informing enants (N = 276)	100	92	96	91	91	95
etters consulting ndividual tenants N = 274)	90	96	97	86	65	90
etters consulting enants' groups N = 67)	85	88	63	55	49	66
eaflets (N = 276)	86	100	81	86	67	83
Handbooks and/or nformation packs N = 275)	91	88	82	52	50	77
dverts/posters/ otices (N = 272)	60	80	48	45	51	54
Newsletters N = 268)	48	38	31	24	14	31
Other means N = 255)	30	19	22	14	19	21

ource: National LA survey

appropriate for particular tenants or groups of tenants. For example, handbooks and information packs are often supplied to individual tenants at the start of their tenancy giving details of the terms of tenancy, emergency repairs numbers and other practical information; while newsletters can provide topical information about plans and changes in housing management, encourage discussion, or invite comments from tenants about matters of current concern.

Letters

The research found that ninety-five per cent of local authorities in England, Scotland and Wales and eighty-nine per cent of housing associations in England used letters as a method of informing their tenants. Similar proportions of authorities (90 per cent) and associations (92 per cent) used letters to consult tenants. The figures (Table 1 and Table 2) show that letters were the most common method of communication, but that the extent of their use varied depending on the purpose and for whom they were intended. This variation was very marked in Scotland where nine out of ten authorities used letters to inform individual tenants, but less than half used them to consult tenants' groups. This may reflect the lack of a legal duty to consult tenants in Scotland.

Leaflets

More than four out of five councils and three out of five housing associations used leaflets as a way of communicating with tenants. All the metropolitan district councils and two-thirds of the Scottish local authorities used this method.

Handbooks and information packs

Nearly as many housing associations provided handbooks and/or information packs for tenants, as used letters. In England the great majority

TABLE 2

Written communications to housing association tenants in England: proportions of associations using different methods

	%
Letters informing tenants (N = 89)	89
Letters consulting individual tenants (N = 74)	92
Letters consulting tenants' groups (N = 74)	51
Leaflets (N = 74)	64
Handbooks and/or information packs (N = 73)	86
Adverts/posters/notices (N = 73)	45
Newsletters (N = 74)	46
Other means (N = 75)	21

Source: HA survey

of councils produced some kind of handbook or information pack compared to only half of the councils in Scotland and Wales. The different legal provisions that apply in Scotland could explain some of this difference. Handbooks can provide information to tenants on everything from how to pay rent and claim housing benefit, to advice on how to go about forming a tenants' association and what to do about racial harassment.

Adverts, posters and notices

Less than half of the housing associations, but more than half of the local authorities used adverts, posters or notices to communicate with tenants. These were placed in the local press and displayed in places such as local libraries.

Newsletters

Just under one-third of local authority housing departments produced a newsletter for tenants, but it is not known how regularly or frequently they were issued. In some cases a tenants' supplement formed part of a more widely distributed council newspaper. Almost half of the housing associations appeared to use newsletters to communicate with tenants.

Surveys

The research found that questionnaire surveys were used by a growing number of authorities and associations as a method of participation. These could range from a small postal questionnaire concerned with a particular issue such as plans for off-street parking, to a large-scale door-to-door household survey looking in depth at tenants' views and attitudes.

One housing association employed researchers to conduct a survey of over 1,500 of its tenants to find out what expectations they had of their landlord at the time and in the future, what they knew about their landlord and the services it provided, and how satisfied tenants were with service provision and delivery.

Other methods

Some local authorities and housing associations used other types of written communication with their tenants. For example, one local authority had produced a consultation document on its housing strategy for the next five years and some Scottish authorities and associations made available copies of their housing plans to tenants or tenants' groups.

Exhibitions and audio-visual aids such as videos were also used.

Landlords used the press and other media to varying degrees as a method of communicating with tenants and a wider public. Some employed press officers, while others used the media in a more ad hoc fashion: for example, occasional letters from the Chief Housing Officer to the local paper.

Face to Face contact

Since 1975, when the last large-scale survey of tenant participation in local authority housing management in England and Wales was carried out (Richardson 1977), the use of participation methods involving face to face or direct contact has increased. The different means by which tenants may participate directly in local authorities or housing associations can be categorised as:

- tenant representation on the housing committee or housing association management committee
- tenant representation on sub-committees of the housing committee or management committee, for example, district committee, area board, management and maintenance sub-committee
- tenant representation on advisory committees or working parties which may report to the housing committee or management committee, but which are not formal sub-committees
- discussion meetings at regular intervals between tenants and council or housing association representatives
- discussion meetings at irregular intervals between tenants and council and housing association representatives.

This is not an exhaustive list but covers the principal methods examined by Richardson and in the Glasgow University surveys.

As with the written word, different **methods** of face to face contact may be part of different **processes** of participation. For example, regular discussion meetings between landlord and tenants' representatives may be part of a process of providing information, dialogue or consultation, (see Chapter Four).

It is useful at this point to distinguish between formal and informal methods of face to face participation. In this guide all categories of face to face contact are regarded as formal participation, apart from irregular discussions between council or housing association representatives and tenants, which are considered as informal participation. Other methods of informal participation exist such as phone calls, or visits by tenants' association committee members to the housing office, or councillors passing on information to tenants on their estate. As these methods are so informal it is not possible to measure the extent and frequency of their use. However, the research indicates that they are most likely to develop where more formal methods of tenant participation already exist.

Tenants on Committees

Just four local authorities (all London boroughs) had arrangements for tenants to sit on their housing committee with full voting rights, (see Table 3), the same number as in Richardson's 1975 survey. The Local Government and Housing Act 1989 abolishes voting rights for tenant co-optees.

Only 22 councils in the survey had arrangements for tenants to be on their housing committee in an advisory or observer capacity, while in other areas there was a right of address for deputations of tenants to the housing committee.

TABLE 3

Number of authorities with tenant representation on council committees

	London Boroughs (N = 20)	Met. Districts (N = 25)	English Non-Met. Districts (N = 165)	Welsh Districts (N = 21)	Scottish Districts (N = 43)	Total (N = 274)
Tenants on Housing Committee with:						
■ full voting power	4	0	0	0	0	4
■ partial voting power	1	1	0	0	0	2
■ advisory role or observer status	2	2	14	1	3	22
Tenants on Sub-Committee with:						
■ full voting power	9	4	5	0	2	20
■ partial voting power	0	0	2	0	1	3
■ advisory role or observer status	4	4	13	0	2	23
■ other	1	1	2	0	0	4

Source: National LA survey

Nearly one-fifth of the housing associations in the Glasgow survey had tenants on their management committees with full voting rights. In 1985 the NFHA found that over a quarter of all housing associations had tenants on their management committees with full voting rights, (Crook, 1985). This indicates that a higher proportion of associations than local authorities involved tenants at the highest level of tenant participation, although Crook's research found that less than one in eight of all associations had more than one tenant on their management committee. Large associations were more likely to have tenant members than were small ones. In one association nearly half of the management committee were tenants elected by tenants or by shareholders.

TABLE 4

Tenant representation on housing association committees in England

	No. of Housing Associations
Tenants' representatives on management committee with:	
■ full voting power	12
■ partial voting power	0
■ advisory role or observer status	7
■ other	7
Tenants' representatives on sub-committee of management committee with:	
■ full voting power	11
■ partial voting power	0
■ advisory role or observer status	5
■ other	3

Source: HA survey (N = 71)

It is not known which is the most widespread method by which tenant representatives are selected to serve on management committees. They may be elected by tenants or chosen by existing members or recommended by staff.

Half of the associations in Crook's survey did not have tenants on their committee at the time and did not want them in the future. This polarisation of attitudes towards tenant involvement in committees was also revealed in interviews with existing committee members. While over half were in favour of this form of tenant involvement, more than one-third were totally opposed to tenant membership of committees and one in five were opposed to any kind of tenant involvement whatsoever.

TABLE 5

Tenant representation on housing association management committees in England

Size of association (units)	Number of tenants on committee		
	0	1	2 or more
	%	%	%
1 – 25	83	12	5
26 – 100	80	13	7
101 – 500	70	17	13
501 – 1000	63	22	15
1001 and over	61	14	24
All associations	73	15	12

Source: Strengthening Committees, Tony Crook, NFHA, 1985

'Housing associations are encouraged to have tenant representatives on management committees, both centrally and at an area level ... Having a 'token tenant' on the management committee, however, if this is the only tenant involvement there is, may do little in real terms towards making associations more responsive to tenant needs. Tenant representatives on management committees should be the visible evidence of broader participation.'

Housing Corporation, 1978

'ASSOCIATIONS ARE EXPECTED TO:

...

1.3 Have a committee and membership that can broadly represent the communities and consumers they serve.'

Housing Corporation, 1989

Tenants on sub-committees

It is possible for tenant representatives to be members of a variety of formal working parties and sub-committees of a council's housing committee or housing association's management committee. This method of participation, although infrequent (see Tables 3 and 4), is more widely used than representation on the housing committee. The survey revealed that metropolitan district councils and London boroughs were much more likely to have tenant representatives on the housing committee and its

In one London borough, tenants' representatives with full voting rights sit on the housing management and technical services sub-committees of the housing committee, as well as working parties of the housing committee formed to consider allocations policy, decentralisation, and tenancy conditions. In this case, tenants are involved in both the monitoring of existing policies and practices, and in proposals for new ones.

TABLE 6

Other methods of face to face contact between councils and tenants

	London Boroughs (N = 20) %	Met. Districts (N = 25) %	English Non-Met. Districts (N = 165) %	Welsh Districts (N = 21) %	Scottish Districts (N = 43) %	Total (N = 274) %
Proportion with:						
Advisory committees	65	32	18	19	21	23
Regular discussion meetings	85	40	27	19	35	35
Irregular discussion meetings	75	72	62	82	74	69
Other	5	4	12	0	2	4

Source: National LA survey

formal sub-committees than were non-metropolitan district councils.

In housing associations tenant representation on sub-committees or working parties is less widespread than on management committees. This may be because few associations have committees of this type, although some do have regional or area committees.

TABLE 7

Other methods of face to face contact between housing associations and tenants in England

	%
Proportion with:	
Advisory committees	15
Regular discussion meetings	30
Irregular discussion meetings	71
Other	10

Source: HA survey (N = 73)

Advisory committees

Nearly a quarter of all local authorities used advisory or liaison committees as a method of tenant participation. Such committees, composed of tenant members and/or officers and/or councillors, usually reported to the council's housing committee. This arrangement was most common among the London boroughs where two-thirds had tenant advisory committees. Approximately one in five of all non-metropolitan

'One of the ten housing associations with successful tenant participation studied by the authors of *Heard or Ignored* had a system of area committees where over half the members were tenants and meetings were usually chaired by a tenant representative. The tenants' formal role was an advisory one, although in practice they exerted considerable influence which was increasing as their experience and confidence grew.'

Platt et al, 1987

district councils had such advisory committees, a level more than six times higher than in Richardson's 1975 survey. Advisory committees with tenant members were less common among housing associations.

Regular discussion meetings

In most non-metropolitan district councils in England, and in parts of Scotland and Wales, tenants appeared to be seldom involved in any formal scheme for direct participation, not even at the level of regular discussion meetings between tenants and the council. However, since 1975 such meetings have become more commonplace in all types of local authority in England and Wales. For example, ten metropolitan district councils now hold regular discussion meetings with tenants' representatives, compared with none in 1975. The proportion of housing associations with arrangements for regular discussion meetings with tenants was even less than for local authorities.

Irregular discussion meetings

Irregular discussion meetings with tenants were the most typical method of face to face participation used by roughly seven out of ten housing associations and local authorities. Their use was especially widespread in Welsh authorities, which may compensate for the lack of formal direct participation. More councils in England and Wales undertook irregular discussions with tenants than before: four in five compared with less than two in five in 1975.

Issues for tenant involvement

Housing associations and authorities varied a great deal in their attitudes and practices as to the range of management matters in which they involved tenants. At one extreme an association or authority might discuss regularly with tenants' representatives any issue that might arise in running a housing organisation, such as building, allocations policies or rent arrears control. In other cases tenants might only be consulted occasionally and over specific issues such as modernisation work or changes to rent collection methods.

The research showed that for local authorities the range of issues open to tenant involvement varied according to the type of authority and the size of its stock. On the whole, London boroughs involved tenants over the widest range of subjects and the Scottish councils over the narrowest. Sales policy was the only matter on which London boroughs were less willing to involve tenants than other authorities. On matters of rents, repairs, allocations and new-build capital projects, substantial differences occurred between types of council in their willingness to involve tenants. Few involved their tenants in such matters as void control, rent levels or arrears policy (see Tables 8 and 9).

There did not seem to be any link between the size of associations and their willingness to encourage tenant participation on certain topics. As with council landlords, housing associations rarely involved tenants in matters of void control and arrears policy. At the time of the survey rent levels were fixed by rent officers and were not subject to an association's discretion.

Modernisation or rehabilitation was the issue most commonly the subject of consultation or involvement by authorities and associations. Tenants in the case study areas, however, also felt that repairs, rents and allocations were important issues.

TABLE 8

Issues on which council tenants were consulted or involved
% of authorities consulting or involving tenants

Issue	London Boroughs %	Met. Districts %	English Non-Met. Districts %	Welsh Districts %	Scottish Districts %	Total %
Modernisation or rehab	90	90	80	76	71	81
New build	65	43	30	10	24	32
Estate management	85	76	64	52	44	63
Tenant consultation policy	85	67	48	38	39	51
Repairs policy	65	48	31	24	27	34
Repairs admin.	60	52	20	14	24	26
Rent collection	50	43	36	19	7	32
Rent levels	45	5	9	0	7	11
Arrears policy	15	14	10	10	10	11
Allocations policy	60	48	24	19	24	29
Allocations admin.	40	29	11	14	10	15
Homelessness policy/advice admin.	30	29	10	0	12	13
Housing aid/advice	25	19	16	0	7	15
Void control	25	24	8	10	12	11
Sales policy	20	29	13	0	5	13

Source: National LA survey (N = 263)

TABLE 9

Issues on which housing association tenants in England were consulted or involved

Issue	% of associations consulting or involving tenants
Modernisation or rehabilitation	60
New build	31
Estate management	72
Tenant consultation policy	49
Repairs policy	46
Repairs administration	37
Rent collection	54
Arrears policy	24
Allocations policy	25
Allocations administration	21
Void control	10
Sales policy	15

Source: HA survey (N = 68)

Modernisation

Four out of five councils involved their tenants on modernisation matters, making it by far the most common issue for tenant participation. The only other topics on which more than half the councils in the survey involved their tenants were estate management and tenant consultation policy.

A smaller proportion of housing associations than local authorities involved tenants in modernisation and rehabilitation, although it was the second most widespread topic for tenant participation. This may reflect the fact that fewer housing associations than local authorities were involved in modernising or rehabilitating properties with tenants in occupation. Estate management was the most usual subject of participation for housing association tenants.

Repairs

Surveys of tenants have frequently shown that repairs cause them most concern, yet only one-third of local authorities involved their tenants in repairs policy and one-quarter in repairs administration. In contrast nearly half of housing associations involved tenants in repairs policy, while more than one-third involved them in repairs administration. The nature of this involvement varied widely and included tenant satisfaction surveys, complaints forums and tenant membership of a repairs working party with full voting powers.

In one urban authority tenants' representatives meet regularly with housing and repairs staff in each district to monitor delivery and planning of the repairs service.

Rents and allocations

No more than one-third of all local authorities involved tenants in rents and allocations. Similarly, less than one-third of housing associations involved tenants in allocations policy and administration, but over half involved them in matters of rent collection.

In some authorities tenants' associations have been consulted over proposed changes to the allocations policy. In one area groups were invited to a seminar to hear about and discuss proposed changes.

Tenants are involved in some local lettings schemes. Their involvement may extend to accompanying prospective tenants when they go to look at a flat or house that has been offered to them. In one authority, local lettings committees operate variations of the allocations policy approved by the authority and administered by the local committee of tenants and staff.

Although rent rises are excluded from the matters secure tenants must be consulted about in England and Wales, nevertheless some authorities in England (and Scotland) hold meetings with tenants' representatives to inform them and consult them about proposed revenue budgets and rent levels.

Levels of participation

Each method of tenant participation may be used at different geographical levels, ranging from the individual house or flat to all the property owned by an authority or association. It is possible to identify five main levels:

- authority/housing association wide
- area/district
- neighbourhood
- block/estate
- individual house/flat.

Depending on who will be affected by a decision, the level at which participation takes place may vary. In some authorities and housing associations, the levels may form a pyramid of participation. In others, participation may only take place at one or two levels, such as on individual estates and authority or association wide, but at no intermediate level.

In one local authority, for example, tenants participate at the individual, estate, district and authority level, but the methods and the processes involved vary between and within levels.

> *'There's a need for estate-based consultation instead of district committees because they don't tackle day to day matters. There still would be a need for area committees, but perhaps not so many, to discuss policy issues.'*
>
> *Tenant*

Authority or association wide

The formal structure for participation at the authority or association level can take many different forms. In one authority participation at this level was largely restricted to the federation of tenants' associations which represented more than half the groups in the area. In another case tenants' representatives were elected to serve on a borough-wide basis. This resulted in the concentration of tenant power in one area of the authority from where many of the tenants who were elected happened to come. Consequently, a new structure was devised whereby each district elected its own representative.

Tenants have been involved in working parties on repairs, allocations, tenancy conditions, system-build and tower blocks, decentralisation and tenant consultation.

In another authority, tenants' associations were excluded from the participation process if they failed to satisfy the criteria for recognition based on the proportion of tenants who were members. Thus, while the structure may be open in principle to tenants from all over the borough, only certain groups were allowed to participate.

Some landlords provide support to a tenants' federation. This can be in the form of revenue funding – enough to employ three or four staff; equipment such as a photocopier, a mini-van; premises and a phone line. In one local authority, the federation is funded through a rent levy of two pence a week which goes straight to the federation and tenants' associations. Tenants may opt out if they wish.

Area or district

The dividing line between tenant participation at area, neighbourhood and estate level is not always clear, depending to some extent on the size of authority or association and the size of an estate. Some large estates will constitute neighbourhoods in their own right.

EXAMPLE OF A DISTRICT BASED TENANT PARTICIPATION STRUCTURE

Each tenants' association recognised by the landlord within a district elects a representative to serve on a district committee. They may also send an observer. Three councillors from local wards are nominated by the Council to be members and three more stand as reserves. The committee may only be chaired by a tenant. Officers attend in an advisory capacity. Items can be referred to the committee by tenants' associations, officers, Housing Committee and other district committees. The district committee may put items on the Housing Committee agenda. Each district elects one of its members who is then co-opted to serve on the Housing Committee with full voting powers.

Neighbourhood

Tenant participation at the neighbourhood level may sometimes be part of the landlord's policy of decentralisation. In some London boroughs, participation at a neighbourhood level is open to a variety of interest groups in the area including, but not exclusively, tenants' associations.

> **One local authority has established neighbourhood forums which are composed of estate or street/block representatives, members from local voluntary groups, people representing particular groups, such as the disabled, carers or ethnic minorities and co-opted members. The forum may monitor and make recommendations on the quality and level of local service provision; prepare and amend budgets for projects in the neighbourhood; and comment on planning applications.**

Block or estate

Nearly one-third of local authorities had introduced some kind of local estate-based initiative with tenant involvement. They tend to be larger authorities, especially London boroughs and the metropolitan district councils, perhaps because they have greater concentrations of difficult to let housing. Initiatives range from small-scale environmental improvements and grounds maintenance to community development projects and estate budgets (Holmes, 1988)

TABLE 10

Estate-based Participation Initiatives

	Authorities undertaking estate initiatives No.	%
London Boroughs	11	55
Metropolitan Districts	13	68
English Non-Met. Districts	38	24
Welsh Districts	5	25
Scottish Districts	13	31
Total	80	31

Source: National LA survey (N = 260)

PEP ESTATE BASED MANAGEMENT BOARDS

Estate management boards are in their early stages. Composed of tenants, councillors and co-optees, they control an estate budget – 'a sum of money separately identified from the Housing Revenue Account for the management and maintenance of an estate, separately accounted for, and under the *control* of a local manager or committee' (PEP). The extent of control given to the board, over matters such as rent collection and lettings may be negotiated.

In Wales and Scotland estate initiatives were more widespread than some forms of authority-wide face to face contact such as representation on the housing committee, sub-committees or advisory committees. This perhaps indicates the greater readiness of local authorities to accept tenant participation as a technique appropriate where other housing management approaches have failed.

Individual tenants

Resource constraints and the amount of time available to staff and tenants affect the extent to which tenant participation is possible at an individual level. Methods involving face to face communication with individual tenants were rarely used except on capital projects. When individual participation did take place, it was usually through written communication.

Several local authorities operate tenants' grant schemes. In one case, tenants in a selected area are offered central heating at a cost of an extra £1 a week on the rent. The offer is made by letter to individual tenants followed by a public meeting. The authority aims to offer central heating to about 1,000 tenants every year. The offer is held open for three months and tenants must agree to having gas-fired central heating.

Tenants' associations

It is impossible to talk about tenant participation without looking at tenants' associations. In any formal arrangement for tenant participation, tenants' associations usually play an important part as a recognised channel for communication between individual tenants and their landlord. Tenants' associations can be seen as a discrete method of, or approach to tenant participation or as playing a part in the methods of participation described earlier in this chapter.

Local authorities and housing associations sometimes did not know that their tenants had formed tenants' associations. In other areas, tenants' associations operated with the recognition of the landlord. Formal recognition could depend on such points as: the proportion of tenants in the area who are members, the adoption of an equal opportunities policy, or the keeping of satisfactory accounts. In many areas, implicit recognition was given to tenants' associations without resort to any monitoring or evaluation.

CRITERIA SUGGESTED BY TPAS (ENGLAND) FOR TENANTS' ASSOCIATION RECOGNITION

'An established tenants' group should be expected to:

- **elect its officers and committee annually at a public meeting**
- **have a bank account, keep proper financial records and produce annual audited accounts**
- **adopt a constitution which provides fair and democratic procedures, including a commitment to equal opportunities**
- **provide evidence that 51 per cent of the tenants in the area they represent are members**
- **hold at least one public meeting a year, and organise special meetings if more than ten members request**
- **hold regular committee meetings with at least 25 per cent open to members**
- **produce records of committee and general meetings**
- **report to and receive feedback from members through newsletters, meetings and informal contact.'**

Two in five housing associations knew of no tenants' associations among their tenants, while most of the rest were aware of no more than five. More than one in four of the local authorities (all district councils) knew of no tenants' associations within their area. Associations appeared to be most numerous in London where more than half the boroughs knew of over twenty associations and in three cases knew of more than one hundred. Few Welsh councils were aware of many associations in their area. The reasons for the low number of tenants' associations in some areas may relate to the availability of support and resources from the landlord.

The most common methods reported by tenants' associations to influence a local authority were contact with the local housing officer and ward councillor. More than nine out of ten tenants' associations had taken this approach. More than three-quarters had distributed newsletters or leaflets, attended council meetings, or held their own public meeting as a way of influencing the local authority. Less orthodox methods such as rent strikes or raising an issue through a branch of a political party were rarely used. Preferred methods of influencing a local authority appeared to be the same, regardless of whether or not the authority encouraged participation.

Support to tenants' associations

Many tenants' associations engaged in a variety of activities of a social or welfare nature and with the aim of improving their housing conditions. The more resources available to them, the more likely it was that they performed a wide range of activities. The levels of assistance provided to tenants' groups was very low and did not match the apparent commitment of councils and housing associations to tenant participation.

One London borough which employs eleven staff to work specifically with tenants' groups, provides tenants' halls and meeting places on many estates; funds the three workers employed by the tenants' federation and provides it with premises and meets its running costs; and gives start-up grants to new tenants' associations.

The English and Welsh non-metropolitan district councils appeared to provide least in the way of support to tenants' groups. None of the Welsh authorities in the survey provided premises or grants, although one in ten employed specialist staff to work with tenants' groups and provided other forms of support. Likewise, few housing associations, large or small, provided support to tenants' associations and only one in twenty employed specialist staff to deal with consultation.

The three resources most frequently mentioned by tenants' groups as ones which they lacked but considered useful were a place to meet, a duplicator or photocopier, and a grant from the local authority.

Overall, over one in three local authorities provided no support to tenants' groups and only seven of the seventy-seven housing associations in the survey provided any kind of assistance. The level of support, as with other measures related to formal tenant participation, seems to be associated with the size of the local, authority's housing stock. Scottish councils and the London boroughs emerge as the most generous, while in Wales only one in ten local authorities provided support to tenants' groups.

References

Centre for Housing Research (1989) *The Nature and Effectiveness of Housing Management in England*, DoE, HMSO, London

Crook Tony (1985) *Strengthening Committees*, NFHA, London

Holmes Chris (1988) *Tenant Involvement on Priority Estates*, Priority Estates Project, London

Housing Corporation (1978) *In the Public Eye*, HC3/78, The Housing Corporation, London

Housing Corporation (1989) *Performance Expectations – Housing Association Guide to Self-Monitoring*, The Housing Corporation, London

Platt Steve, Piepe Rita and Smyth Judith (1987) *Heard or Ignored*, NFHA, London

THE PROCESS OF PARTICIPATION

CHAPTER 4

This chapter considers what is going on in the various processes of tenant participation. It is based largely on case studies of tenant participation in six local authorities, supplemented with information on housing associations mainly derived from Heard or Ignored *(Platt et al, 1987).*

process Participation can involve a range of possible processes:

- **providing information** to tenants
- **seeking information** from tenants
- **listening** to the unsolicited views of tenants
- **consulting** tenants – asking them for their views
- **dialogue, negotiation and bargaining** – where tenants are able to influence decisions to varying degrees in a two-way process
- **joint management** – sharing decision-making and responsibility with tenants
- **choice** – from a set of options
- **control** – decision-making by tenants

These processes should not be viewed as a hierarchy, as if in some ladder of participation. They may often overlap and at any one time, several processes may be going on. For example, a public meeting on a modernisation programme may raise issues unrelated to the project, such as tenants' views on an imminent rent increase, to which officers and councillors may respond.

Each process may involve tenants as individuals or as representatives. It may occur only once or it may be part of a continuing relationship between landlord and tenant. It may occur within a formal structure for participation or, in some cases, it may happen informally.

Providing information to tenants

Providing information to tenants is a prerequisite for tenant participation. If tenants are poorly or wrongly informed, they will not be able to participate fully in housing matters. Officers, councillors, committee members and tenants all consider the provision of information of vital importance.

'Tenants are at a disadvantage because knowledge is power. Initially if an authority does not want to encourage them [tenants' associations], they can murder them with the sort of statements they can make, "You can't do that because of this, that or the other." It's one of the easiest statements in the world to make.'

Officer

If tenants think that they are being deliberately misinformed, they may refuse to participate at all in the future.

'Be honest, be open and discuss everything. That's the worst thing of all when people lie or are underhand and they say these things off the top of their head without even batting an eyelid.'

Tenant

'I don't think a lot happens without the tenants knowing. Although negotiations at senior officer level may not always reach them, the place leaks like a sieve.'

Tenant Participation Officer

'Tenants are not as gullible as they were twenty, thirty years ago. They won't have the wool pulled over their eyes.'

Tenant

Where projects, such as modernisation schemes, are in progress, officers sometimes forget that tenants wish to be informed, even when there is nothing to report. The fact that there is no news, *is* news.
Compare

'What about the newsletter? That's another way to keep people informed. What happened to that? Another case of you [officers] not keeping your promises.'

Tenant at modernisation meeting

with

'Meetings are normally every six weeks. I think they're brilliant . . . It takes me an hour to read the papers. They are simple,

single-sentence reports with no verbiage. There are minutes, an area team report, and simple statistics on development, management and maintenance.'

Tenant on area committee
(quoted in Platt et al, 1987)

While providing information to tenants is essential to the development of tenant participation, its value in fostering that development depends on where it comes in the decision-making process: whether tenants are informed at the planning stage of a project, or when all the decisions have been taken and the plan is a fait accompli.

'It's a shame really that in most cases, tenants aren't informed of any improvement. They've just been told, like ourselves "Oh, this is happening", when it's been decided.'

Estate Officer

Letters are the most widely used method of informing housing association and council tenants. As with other forms of written communication they are often a haphazard method of providing information. For example, although all of our case study authorities said that they used letters to inform individual tenants, in one authority thirteen per cent of tenants said that the authority had used this method, while in another more than half said that letters had been used. Factors such as where and how written communication is distributed, relevance, use of plain English or other languages where appropriate, and a clearly identifiable house style may influence the impact it has on tenants (Goodlad, 1986). Communication studies indicate that people are more receptive, the more personalised a piece of written communication is (NCC, 1980).

Tenants who recalled receiving a range of written information – letters, leaflets, newsletters, information packs or handbooks, adverts, posters or notices – considered them to be of roughly equal usefulness. It is possible that confusing or misleading information may generate additional costs and demands on staff time, while irrelevant or inappropriate written communication will waste resources and the time of staff and tenants.

Public meetings and meetings with tenants' associations or their representatives are sometimes more appropriate than written communication alone, as they give the opportunity for discussion and questions and the use of visual aids which thus enables tenants to gain a more thorough understanding of the information. Such meetings can also enlist the assistance of tenants' representatives in informing other tenants.

The effectiveness of information provision depends on the quantity and quality of the material made available. Sometimes tenants may feel swamped by information, if too much is provided at once. Tenants can also be put off participating by the use of jargon, which they may not understand.

> *'I think that the information they [officers] try to get across in an evening is too much.'*
>
> *Tenant on District Committee*

> *'. . . the information must be simple and in every-day language. The speakers should be handpicked, warm, friendly, and able to relate to other people. They don't want to know about HAG, they want to know what their housing association is and what it can do. Start there.'*
>
> *Tenant*
> *(quoted in Platt et al, 1987)*

> *'The word for this council is devious. For example, the reports they send to district committees. A lot of those are just not possible for a normal person to understand. People aren't used to dealing with Council reports. The times they've given a commitment to write simply, they don't. I think it's deliberate.'*
>
> *Tenant*

> *'The architect shut us up and made us feel stupid.'*
>
> *Tenant*

Where a landlord decides to provide information to tenants, it is necessary to be clear about the purpose of the information and for whom it is intended. In many cases it is likely that both written and face to face communication is required. In addition, tenants will sometimes want access to alternative sources of information. Landlords who support participation most enthusiastically tend also to provide resources for tenants' associations to enable them to pay for their own advisers. Landlords who feel that tenants should not seek independent information should bear in mind that this attitude is less likely to engender trust between landlord and tenants than one which acknowledges the tenants' as well as the landlords' rights to seek independent advice.

Seeking information from tenants

Seeking information from individual tenants or groups of tenants is usually an integral part of tenant participation. Some housing officers see tenant participation mainly in these terms, whether through the formal structure of an area or district committee of tenants, or through less formal day to day contact between tenants and the local estate officer.

'It depends how the estate manager uses them [tenants' associations]. They are very beneficial if you have a good rapport with them. They can give you the truth of what's going on which is often difficult if you don't live on the estate.'

Estate Officer

'If you build up a relatively good relationship with tenants and tenants' associations within your own ward, they will feed problems to you. It means that you can get a far clearer picture of what's going on and also it's useful to be able to go along to their meetings and to hear from tenants on the ground what their problems are and what's actually concerning them.'

Councillor

The best method for seeking information depends on what the landlord is looking for. Information about what is happening on an estate or in an area is often obtained through informal personal communication between tenants and officers.

'You can sort out one thing with just one person ringing you. If they're a good tenants' association and people on the estate feel they can trust them, I get to know things very quickly which otherwise would slip by.'

Estate Officer

Some officers seek information from tenants' groups on subjects such as squatting or neighbour disputes, recognising that they are especially well-placed to provide such details. Sometimes it may be necessary to seek information more widely, for example where information is sought from an all-white tenants' association about incidents of racial harassment.

'It may not be the thing to call tenants customers, but it's a basic philosophy of business to find out what people want.'

District Manager

Landlords are increasingly using methods such as surveys and questionnaires or leaflets with tear-off return slips to obtain details about tenants' circumstances and their satisfaction with aspects of the housing service. In the case studies, one in eight tenants said that they would like their landlord to use surveys. These can, however, be an expensive method of collecting tenants' views; other means, such as asking groups of tenants or tenants' associations for their opinions, may be just as effective.

Seeking information may mean identifying areas of need in planning for the future, or monitoring and measuring current standards of provision. It is also a way of showing tenants that the landlord is genuinely interested in their situation and may help to foster other kinds of tenant involvement. But the views of tenants may not always be welcome, with potentially disastrous consequences when the views of tenants are next sought.

> *'We have major structural problems ... but nothing was ever done ... Three years ago the housing manager wrote to say that she didn't want to see us and wanted the monthly meetings stopped. The residents association folded.'*
>
> *Chairperson of Housing Association Sub-committee (quoted in Platt et al, 1987)*

Listening

Listening to the views of tenants and being seen to listen is an essential part of the process of tenant participation. Tenants may provide information and express their views in a variety of forums about a wide range of housing matters. Being prepared to listen to their views can assist the development of good relations between tenant and landlord and encourage tenant participation.

> *'The thing that will foster it [tenant participation] more than anything else is a willingness to listen. If people can see that you're willing to take into account what they say and to change part of what you do, because of what they say, they're going to come forward. You can have tenants on the Housing Committee, all the formal consultation you like, but if you don't listen to them, they're going to be a waste of time and that'll be picked up by the tenants very quickly.'*
>
> *Councillor*

> *'We had a meeting of residents which I chaired ... I was very moved by the whole thing. I hadn't realised how hopeless they were and how little control they had. All the aggression was because they were floundering.'*
>
> *Chairperson of Housing Association Sub-committee (quoted in Platt et al, 1987)*

Being available and accessible to tenants and their representatives is one way to demonstrate a readiness to listen. Some housing officers give tenants' association committee members their direct line telephone number and welcome regular contact with them.

Willingness to listen to tenants' views may itself develop as a result of the introduction of arrangements for tenant participation and the growth of tenant involvement in housing matters.

'I'm sure I've seen the officers' point of view change: more to sort of listening to what we have to say and realising that we're not just a lot of dimwits who have come along to moan about something. Most people have got practical suggestions to make.'

Tenant

If tenants feel that their views are listened to and then ignored, they may be discouraged from expressing their opinions in the future.

'Some [TAs] struggled on, but most disappeared – not because the facilities were stopped, but they were actively discouraged. There was no follow-up from the things the tenants' associations were trying to do. They got the feeling they were banging their heads against a brick wall.'

Tenant

Feedback, follow-up and action are ways of letting tenants know that they are being listened to. Newsletters, regular progress reports at meetings with tenants, and clear explanations of why action has been delayed or rejected can help perform this task.

Listening may involve giving tenants the opportunity to put items on the agenda at meetings with officers, rather than expecting tenants only to discuss subjects of concern to the landlord. Some housing officers, councillors and committee members think that the landlord should be prepared to listen to any views or ideas that tenants have, however unpopular or irrelevant they may seem.

'They [TAs] might come up with ideas that run counter to council policy. I don't see any harm in that either. Council policy's not always necessarily right. It might be at the time. Some council policy when we came, it was stuff that'd been operating since the war.'

Councillor, ex-Chairperson of Housing Committee

'... don't be surprised that, initially, their [tenants'] concern is with immediate problems rather than general questions.'

Housing Association Director
(quoted in Platt et al, 1987)

'I feel that whatever it is their beef, whatever it is their complaint, it should be looked at. No matter how large or how small. Whatever their complaint is, "yes, OK, we'll look into that, we'll come back and ... hopefully [find] a solution as soon as possible."'

Estate Officer

> *'I am concerned that the few, who are vocal don't represent the wide spectrum. But that's no different from any other walk of life.'*
>
> *Housing Association Director*
> *(quoted in Platt et al, 1987)*

It is unfortunate when officers stop listening to the views of a tenant or group of tenants because they think that they are self-interested, or politically motivated, or the officers simply do not like the individuals involved. Officers should normally be concerned with the issues raised rather than the motives or the personalities of the participants.

> *'A tenant member [of a management committee] is entitled to raise what is his own personal interest if this interest also raises general questions, for example, the association not complying with its obligations as a landlord.'*
>
> *Association Committee Member (non-tenant)*
> *(quoted in Platt et al, 1987)*

Listening to tenants' views assists the continuation of tenant participation in housing where it already exists, and helps to foster the development of tenant involvement where it has not been encouraged in the past. Where the landlord does not listen, tenants may lose heart and tenant participation collapse.

Consultation

Consultation is the process of asking tenants for their views in order to consider them before a decision is made.

> *'You've got to be willing to take into account what they [tenants] say. If you haven't got the commitment that says – I am interested, I want to know because it will change my mind in some cases – don't bother.'*
>
> *Councillor*

Local authorities and housing associations in England and Wales are under a duty to consult secure tenants over proposed changes in matters of housing management that will substantially affect them and to take tenants' views into consideration. In practice, the topics for consultation, the level at which it occurs, and the methods used vary widely both between local authorities and between housing associations.

The most widespread subject of tenant consultation is modernisation, possibly because it is an area where landlords clearly see its advantages.

> *'Nothing's done now in this borough without the officers knowing not only what is required for the future, but what the tenants want*

now. They're very careful about that and how the thing is phased in and how it's done. That's all done through consultation from beginning, stage one, to when the builders move out.'

Councillor

'At the end of the day, they're the people that live there ... If you are going to work on their properties, it's just as easy for them to turn round and say what they want. It may well be that somebody living by a railway track would want double-glazed windows as opposed to new sink units and a new bathroom. So I think that they should have quite a heavy say in what's going to happen. It comes back to spending money wisely.'

Estate Officer

From the survey of council tenants, it appears that many tenants are unaware that their landlord makes any attempt to consult them. The most common method used was letters, and tenants appeared to be most aware of this and public meetings as methods of information provision, although this varied both between and within the local authorities. Some landlords are enthusiastic about the value of using self-completed questionnaires and returnable tear-off slips as a method of consulting tenants. However, such methods yield widely varying response rates both between and within landlords. It appears, from the surveys, that the more local and immediate the subject of consultation, the greater the response will be. No one method of consultation can be sufficient if the aim is to consult all tenants.

'As to how you consult, there are a range of options depending on the circumstances, the issue and what suits the people. On some estates, where there's an association, it's legitimate to consult the tenants' associations. Elsewhere, it has to be done by letter.'

Director of Housing

Whichever method is used, it is essential to provide tenants with sufficient time to respond. Time may be required, for example, to read and consider a complex report, seek advice, issue a newsletter, hold a public meeting and frame a response.

On matters of very local concern, small and informal meetings appear to work well. Both tenants and officers may be intimidated by large public meetings where tenants sit in rows facing a line of officers. Such meetings are better at informing than consulting.

Tenants can be put off attending meetings if they are at an inconvenient time, are held in an inaccessible place, or fail to provide a crèche. They may be encouraged to come if there is good publicity (including the use of ethnic minority languages), help with transport and child care, and the subject of consultation is one that they consider relevant.

Tenants and officers do not always agree on what they mean by consultation. Their different views may be due to the stage in the decision-making process at which tenants' opinions are taken into account, and whether or not tenants think that these are seriously considered.

Compare

> ***'Hopefully, we'll get an idea from you what you're views are. We're going to present you with a range of options. It's not a fait accompli.'***
>
> ***District Manager***

with

> ***'They need to consult much earlier. They tend to decide to do something and then tell us, say "This is what we're going to do, what do you think?" Instead of saying "Somebody's suggested that we might like to modernise 'Y' estate. How do you think it should be done? What in your opinion needs to be done? How can we spend 'X' amount on each property?"'***
>
> ***Tenant***

Consulting tenants about plans for change in a particular area may encourage more tenants to participate in the future. Where a landlord has not previously consulted tenants, it may take time for tenants to believe that the landlord is now committed to consultation.

> ***'I'm finding now that people are learning to respond more than they did previously, because I think word's getting round that if they don't, they're going to miss out on things, and when we consult now, we really mean it.'***
>
> ***District Manager***

The process of consultation does not end with the last public meeting, or on receipt of the last tenant questionnaire. Landlords need to ensure that tenants' views are considered and that tenants are informed of decisions taken and the reasons why tenants' views may not have been accepted.

Dialogue, negotiation and bargaining

A process involving dialogue, negotiation or bargaining is one where both tenants and landlord exert an influence on decisions in a two-way flow of communication, during which the extent of the tenants' influence may vary over time. It often takes place within the setting of a formal structure for participation, such as a working party or liaison committee where tenants are members and derive some power from their membership. Tenants are nearly always acting as representatives of associations or of the tenants in their area, street or block. When it happens informally, this can be through informal contacts between tenants and the landlord or through the use of the media.

Dialogue, negotiation and bargaining cannot occur where tenants have no power. One method that landlords have used to equalise the balance of power is to provide tenants with access to independent advice. In one borough where tenants' representatives sat on a tenancy agreement working party, they were helped by the council to pay for advice from the local law centre. Direct financial support to tenants' associations to cover running costs may also assist dialogue and negotiation by providing the means by which an association can sustain itself in what may be a long drawn-out process.

A process of dialogue, negotiation or bargaining implies some flexibility on the part of both tenants and landlord and a willingness to change. If landlord and tenants hold entrenched views, then there is little opportunity for dialogue.

> ***'I think that's the place where you can be constructive, before people's minds are made up. It's the point where you can have a constructive dialogue. Once peoples' minds are made up, all you do is have an argument.'***
>
> **Councillor**

> ***'How does an officer see himself? [sic] Does he see himself as representing the landlord managing the estates, or does he see it as a two-way thing if you've got an idea and you want support for it, and they've [tenants] got an idea and they want support for it, surely there's somewhere you can meet in the middle, if not take one idea altogether?'***
>
> **Councillor**

Dialogue, negotiation or bargaining may result in conflict or consensus. Conflict is less likely where all participants are clear about the subject and purpose of participation.

> ***'When you've got an homogeneous group like tenants, then I think you've got to work in partnership with them. They must understand that, as well as you must understand it. They can't expect you to do everything that they want you to do, just as I wouldn't expect them to do everything I wanted them to do.'***
>
> **Councillor**

'Area committees (with tenants in the majority) have no formal delegated powers. The management committee has to ratify their decisions, but in practice will delegate most things ... tenants influence things in a direct and dynamic way. If there is a problem they will home in on it every time they meet until it is resolved.'

Director of a Housing Association (quoted in Platt et al, 1987)

Almost by definition some conflict is inevitable in a process of dialogue, negotiation or bargaining. It does not necessarily lead to the breakdown of tenant participation and it does not have to be avoided. Where participation is most firmly established tenants and landlords readily agree to disagree on occasion and move on to the next issue.

'If you take the case in this block, in 'Z' they [the tenants] were arguing for an inappropriate technical solution and it actually needed some considerable time arguing back and forth, having meetings with tenants, having meetings with officers and political parties, to arrive at a consensus that would allow things to be taken forward.'

Councillor

'I think you will get conflict. I don't see that you can avoid it, besides conflict brings change.'

Councillor

Joint management

Only a small number of landlords have entered into joint management, which involves the sharing of responsibility and decision-making between tenant and landlord. Sometimes tenants are given responsibilities, which are not matched with any real power to make decisions. For example, where tenants were co-opted members of a council housing committee, they shared responsibility with councillors and risked equally with them the possibility of surcharge. However, the extent to which they were able to share in decision-making is unclear, if final decision-making powers rested with the full council from which they were excluded.

'It's a great step forward [tenant representatives on the Housing Committee], but they're so outnumbered. Even when you win a decision, they get put back to the Council.'

Tenant

In any process of joint management, such as tenant co-option on to a housing committee, it is important to maintain informal methods of tenant participation, so that those tenants outside the formal mechanism of participation can participate if they wish.

> *'I like the idea of tenants co-opted on to committees but I would still like informal methods to exist, because those people co-opted on to committees, just like any structure, they would become sort of elitist. They wouldn't set out to be, it is just an inevitable outcome of involvement. You're the one there with other people, you've got all the information and it is very difficult not to get into the role that you're the one that's taking decisions. If you don't keep the consultation going, they will become just like other councillors.'*
>
> *Councillor*

Most processes of joint management involve powers to share decisions on the allocation of resources. Tenants seem much more likely to participate where this process takes place.

> *'If you gave them [District Committees] a budget that they could play with. Not necessarily to do major things like council repairs, but stuff like they've always wanted to get this gate fixed, or they wanted some of that fencing put up, or that land relaid ... or whatever; the thing began to expand as it went on.'*
>
> *Councillor*

> *'One of the real advantages of going to the District Committees is that you can get some things done. For instance, this year we're getting the ceilings painted in the garages and some unnecessary walls taken down.'*
>
> *Tenant*

In a process of joint management, the initiative does not lie only with tenants. The attitudes of participants are crucially important: all must be willing to take some responsibility but be equally willing to share it. This requires an equalising of the relationship between tenants, officers and members of the housing or management committee. Where this happens no one group controls the agenda; each idea is considered on its merits.

> *'Participation is where an idea comes from whatever source – it can be the tenants, it can be from anybody – officers, councillors, it could be anybody. And you take that idea and with everybody involved: councillors, officers and the tenants in a joint venture, you take that to its fruition or not if it is not a workable idea, but you flesh it out and see if it works.'*
>
> *Tenant Participation Officer*

To establish an equal relationship between tenants and landlord in a process of joint management, landlords can help by providing support and advice to tenants. In one local authority tenant participation officers are members of improvement project teams along with tenants, other officers and councillors. They act as advocates for and advisers to the tenants, ensuring that tenants have access to the information that they need to participate equally on the project teams.

Choice

Tenants may choose from options in a one-off process of participation. It may be choice by a group of tenants or by tenants individually. Where tenants are provided with a choice, it may be at the end of a period of consultation or other participation process, or it may be after many decisions have already been made by the landlord alone.

Choice is most frequently offered in modernisation and improvement schemes (IoH/RIBA, 1988). For instance, tenants may be able to choose colours for new front doors or select from a menu of possible improvements which particular combination they would like. Even though the options may often be very limited, tenants seem to appreciate having some choice as it allows them a say in matters which directly affect them.

> ***'We got a choice of windows, but when it came down to it, you didn't really have a choice, because the other two choices weren't that good anyway ... Nevertheless, they are asking you about it anyway.***
>
> ***Tenant***

> ***'I like the way now they consult people about their modernisation and allow people to have a bit of choice in how it's done ... When they put in our central heating system, each house was able to choose where they wanted the radiators put which was much easier for the tenants. We are able to choose where we wanted our radiators and that was nice.'***
>
> ***Tenant***

Control

Control is a process where tenants take responsibility and make some decisions. Limited control may exist in tenant management co-operatives, while greater control occurs in ownership co-operatives. Other processes of tenant participation are sometimes seen as preparing the way for control. However, some tenants' associations see a clear distinction between their activities and those of co-operatives. Not every tenant wants to participate in all the processes of participation. Where landlords are genuinely committed to participation, they recognise this and see tenant control as part of the range of processes which constitute tenant participation.

> *'Some [tenants] want a bit of an involvement, some want a bit more than that. You can go through the whole spectrum and you say there's going to be some at the very top end of the scale who want to run the whole damn thing themselves, and I don't think there should be a reason why we should discourage them. If that's what they want, let them have it.'*
>
> *Councillor*

However, some doubts remain.

> *'[The] disadvantage of tenant participation is that you could lose absolute control. Perhaps that's no bad thing, perhaps that's an advantage.'*
>
> *Councillor*

> *'We don't need to be frightened of tenant involvement as long as we are sure tenants can't take over. We have a one third rule which keeps them in their place. You couldn't have a rabble of tenants taking over, you never know where it would lead.'*
>
> *Committee Member*
> *(quoted in Platt et al, 1987)*

Some tenants think that without some control, there are decisions they should not be asked to make.

> *'We don't have input into the decisions that really affect our lives. [We] can only go to the District Committees. We don't have total responsibility over running of the estate. If we did, we could vote for a rent increase.'*
>
> *Council Tenant*

A common objection to tenant control is that tenants will not operate a fair allocations policy, and that they could discriminate against black and ethnic minority applicants. There is, however, no evidence to substantiate this view. On the other hand, several studies have been carried out, by the Commission for Racial Equality among others, of local authorities' allocations policies and practices which have revealed both institutional and direct discrimination. Thus, objections to tenant control on the grounds that tenants will be biased in their allocations is not a sufficient reason on its own to oppose the idea.

References

Goodlad Robina (1986) *Telling the Tenants*, Scottish Consumer Council, Glasgow

National Consumer Council (1980) *Gobbledygook*, NCC, London

Platt Steve, Piepe Rita, Smyth Judith (1987) *Heard or Ignored*, NFHA London

Institute of Housing and Royal Institute of British Architects (1988) *Tenant Participation in Housing Design*, IoH and RIBA, London

THE PARTICIPANTS

CHAPTER 5

This chapter is concerned with the people involved in tenant participation. It discusses the variety of roles played by housing officers, tenants and management committee or council members, and examines how the skills, attitudes and motivations of the actors can influence the participation process.

Officers The officer's role varies depending on the type of participation process in which he or she is involved. Officers may act as communicator, adviser, or trainer, or some combination of these three.

As a basic requirement the nature of the process and the officer's role in it need to be made explicit, as officers are sometimes unclear and confused about what is expected of them.

> ***'You need to tell us exactly what's expected of us as estate officers, because then we'd meet with them [tenants' associations] on a more regular basis.'***
>
> *Estate Officer*

Officers as communicators

Communication is an essential feature of participation. It is, therefore, important that officers are both willing and able to communicate with tenants whether in writing or in face to face situations. Officers need to be able to use plain English and to avoid the use of jargon and technical terms. If tenants have a limited knowledge of English, landlords should consider employing officers with appropriate language skills and should provide translations of written material and interpreters at meetings or request the assistance of local ethnic minority organisations or community groups.

It is sometimes assumed that tenants alone lack skills in verbal communication. But some officers have difficulty in expressing themselves clearly and lack confidence in public speaking. Training and support for officers can assist the development of these skills, but is seldom made available.

> ***'Every officer should be able to communicate with the public and a lot of them can't. A lot can't speak and they're not very good at putting things forward. There should be some kind of training in that.'***
>
> ***Tenant***

An officer's ability to communicate well with tenants may be influenced by their attitude towards tenants and tenant participation. Some officers see tenant participation as a nuisance and an obstacle to efficient management. Others think that it may undermine their position and authority as housing managers. Officers with these negative and defensive attitudes may be unwilling or slow to communicate with tenants. Senior officers can play a part here by appointing officers who are sympathetic to tenant participation, and by setting an example through their own work of the kind of relationship which they want with tenants and tenants' groups.

The development of tenant participation may be obstructed by officers who lie to tenants or mislead them by promising things that they cannot deliver. Tenants respect honesty in officers, even if it means being told things they do not want to hear.

> ***'It's no good saying, "I'll take down your shopping list of 35 items", and come back at the next meeting and say, "I'm sorry Mr X, I've been told by someone else, none of these are on." Better to tell them there and then.'***
>
> ***District Manager***

Another aspect of the officer's role as communicator is the importance of responding and giving feedback to tenants. Tenants are often frustrated by the length of time it takes for officers to answer requests for information or to implement decisions in which they have had a say.

> ***'We tenants, we go to our District Committees, say what we want, but nothing happens. Things are put in front of us; we say our comments and nothing happens.'***
>
> ***Tenant***

Some officers voice concern about the representativeness of tenants' associations. However, where officers hold this view, it is not always translated into an attempt to communicate with a wider group of tenants, but may be used instead as a justification for ignoring the existing tenants' association. If there is genuine concern that a tenants' group does not reflect the composition or views of an area, (for example, an all-white tenants' association on an estate with many black tenants), then the officer as communicator should be looking at ways of reaching a greater number of tenants or tenants more representative of the local community. To avoid upsetting the existing tenants' group, it may be most useful to try to work with the group, providing funds and other support to help them expand their membership.

Officers may have a variety of motives for believing in the value of tenant participation. Where their attitude is a positive one, they are more likely to be willing to communicate with tenants and tenants' groups. However, willingness is not a substitute for the ability to communicate. Officers need a combination of both motivation and ability.

Officers as advisers

Officers may act as advisers to tenants participating in housing management, giving advice on questions such as the most suitable constitution, whom to approach in the council or housing association, or what range of policy options exist over a particular problem. This function may be better performed by staff with a specific brief to work with tenants and tenants' groups, but, whether or not such specialist staff are employed, all officers in contact with tenants should be prepared to act as advisers. When an officer combines the role of adviser to tenants and tenants' groups with that of the landlord's agent, he or she may face a conflict of role. The interests of tenant and landlord do not always coincide and this may put the officer in a difficult position and jeopardise the development of tenant participation. It is in such situations that the arguments seem clearest in favour of keeping the two roles separate. The danger is that by splitting the two roles, those responsible for developing tenant participation may become marginalised.

Local authorities and housing associations may either employ specialist tenant participation officers themselves, or they may provide funds to outside bodies to do so. In the latter case, the tenant adviser or advocate may have greater independence, but is disadvantaged by having less access to information and to housing officers.

> *'We've been really lucky with the tenant participation officers. They've got us furniture for the hall and help like that. They know how to apply for grants, because we had nothing in the hall. We had no tea urn, no crockery, no anything. So we applied for a grant and we got that.'*
>
> Tenant

When officers play the part of advisers, it is important they do not try to change roles when tenants do not take their advice or do not ask for it.

> *'I see the role of this service as to work with tenants and to discuss with them areas where they can realistically campaign and to advise them, not actually stop them where they've got a no-go area. In other words, that that wouldn't work, but this may. That's advising. It's saying at the end of the day, it's down to you. Well I've seen some officers really incensed because they've been told "No, you're not invited to this meeting. We want to meet on our own", and feel really slighted because they haven't got this automatic right to what, in effect, is a private meeting. I came from the tenants' movement, I only go to meetings I'm invited to because that's how I would feel.'*
>
> *Tenant Participation Officer*

> *'I contacted the tenant participation officer and took an instant dislike to him. He was saying "I'll do this and I'll do that." And so I said "No, I just want to see what the set up is, I'll do it myself."'*
>
> *Tenant*

Officers as trainers

The officer's role as trainer in tenant participation has not been widely developed. Informally, officers may provide training to tenants, other officers and members on a range of subjects. Where the role has been formalised, it has been officers with a specific responsibility for developing tenant participation who have usually acted as trainers. This does not have to be the case. Officers can provide different types of training, for example: practical skills such as book-keeping or newsletter production; housing expertise relating to matters such as housing law or finance; and role-training, preparing tenants or officers for a particular role in a tenant participation scheme. Officers can also promote training by arranging for it to be carried out by others, such as community workers or the Workers Educational Association.

Few estate officers themselves receive training on tenant participation and their role in it. As a result, some do not always see working with tenants and tenants' groups as a high priority or as something to be encouraged. Training, encouragement, and the good example of more senior staff, is needed to dispel their fears and uncertainties so that they are clear about what is expected of them, and develop the skills to facilitate tenant participation.

Councillors and management committee members

Councillors and management committee members, like housing officers, have a role to play in tenant participation as communicators, advisers and enablers. Whether and how they perform these roles depends on their skills, attitudes and motivations. Although some officers thought that councillors and management committee members should not be involved in tenant participation, tenants' representatives considered that it was important that both officers and policy makers were involved. For example, the survey showed that almost as many tenants' groups contacted their ward councillor at some time over a year, as contacted the local estate officer.

Members as communicators

As communicators, councillors and management committee members may provide a channel for the flow of information between tenants and landlord. Their role tends to be an informal one, such as attending tenants' association meetings or liaison committees on modernisation programmes. As policy-makers, councillors and management committee members have a special part to play in communicating with tenants on policy issues. The skills and attitudes needed for the role of communicator are similar to those needed by officers in that role.

> ***'I remember once when a tenant representative asked what some letters stood for, one or two of the committee members began to use ordinary language but they forgot again by the next meeting.'***
> *Tenant, ex-member of Management Committee*

Where councillors or management committee members are hostile to tenant participation, they can successfully obstruct it by refusing to communicate with tenants. Where officers are hostile, councillors and management committee members who are sympathetic may act as mediators between tenants and officers.

Members as advisers

Councillors and management committee members can play an active part in encouraging tenants' associations and providing them with advice and guidance: from how to get started and apply for funds, to what the landlord's policy is on a particular subject and how to go about changing it.

> ***'[Councillors] should be there to give advice and guidance to tenants' associations on the council policies that they're setting.'***
> ***Estate Officer***

Councillors, in particular, because of their political experience and expertise may be in a good position to give advice to tenants' groups on tactics and strategies in a process of negotiation and bargaining. But not all councillors or committee members will be willing to assist groups whose aims they do not support. In these circumstances the role of officers assumes even greater importance.

Members as enablers

As policy makers with fiscal powers, councillors and management committee members may decide to introduce a tenant participation policy and allocate resources for its implementation. In this way, they may enable the development of tenant participation by giving a clear sign to officers of what is expected of them.

Whether councillors and management committee members assist the introduction and growth of tenant participation depends on their attitude to it. Management committee members of housing associations are generally in favour, but may oppose particular *forms* such as having tenants on the committee (Platt et al, 1987). Although councillors mean different things by tenant participation, none of the councillors in the study were totally opposed to the idea. Some saw tenant participation as a political strategy, others saw it as an element of good practice in housing management.

> ***'I don't believe that housing departments and councillors know everything . . . the input by tenants in many cases is very important. It helps to shape decisions, it can also help to be economic in housing. I think it plays a vital part. I have always been one for consultation.'***
>
> ***Councillor***

Some councillors and management committee members regard tenant participation as conflicting with their own role, especially where tenants have voting rights on committees.

> ***'We've got councillors and you can tell straight away from their attitude, they don't want tenants telling them what they think of their policy, or they've made a bad decision. They don't want that at all.'***
>
> ***Councillor***

> ***'Just over half the committee members were in favour of having tenants on the committee. However, over one-third were totally opposed to it.'***
>
> ***(Platt et al, 1987)***

Tenants' associations

There are widely conflicting views held about the roles of tenants' groups by tenants and landlords involved in tenant participation. Some of this variation is due to differences of view about the purpose of participation. Roles that have been identified include:

- providing expert local knowledge and information to the landlord
- identifying issues of concern
- suggesting solutions to problems
- representing the views and interests of tenants to the landlord and other bodies
- providing information to tenants
- acting as an agent for housing management
- campaigning for changes or improvements in housing policy or practice or other matters
- acting as a focus for political activity
- organising social and welfare activities
- working for the development of the community.

Many of these roles are essentially about communication, which can occur in either direction.

> ***'I think they're [tenants' associations] there to highlight to the council any problem on the estate and they're a place to go to if they feel that they're not getting the satisfaction from the council. The tenants' associations can liaise with the council on their behalf. They're also there to bring any idea, after all they've got to live on the estate and if they feel that there's anything that they can bring to the attention of the council that can better the condition of the estate, that is what they're there for.'***
>
> ***Estate Officer***

There is a tendency among officers to view the communication role of tenants' groups mainly in terms of the communication between the tenants' group and the landlord. Sometimes tenants' groups are criticised for being unrepresentative. In such cases the landlord may be concerned about the degree of communication between the tenants' groups and ordinary tenants. There may be ways that the landlord can help tenants' groups to perform this role by providing training and resources. Given their limited resources and dependence on voluntary help, it may be asking too much of tenants' groups to expect them to communicate with all tenants in their area. After all, landlords themselves rarely do this.

The role of tenants' groups is not always clear. They may want to have a say in housing management policy and practice, but sometimes feel that they and their representatives are being used to do the landlord's job

> ***'My wife says I'm always doing the council's work. I'm a glorified estate officer, caretaker and everything else.'***
> ***Tenants' Association Chairperson***

Tenants' groups may be reluctant to take on responsibilities which were previously the landlord's, if they believe that they still have no say in the decisions which affect those responsibilities.

Some officers criticise tenants' associations for taking on a political role. In the survey of tenants' associations, only one in seven mentioned political campaigning as among their main activities. Less than one in five tenants agreed with the view that tenants' associations are too political. It seems that sometimes the political affiliation of individual members of a tenants' group is ascribed to the group as a whole. When this happens the group may be labelled as a political organisation although its actual aims and activities may be apolitical.

Tenants' groups may also have other roles quite separate from their relationship with the landlord. Social and welfare activities are important elements in the work of most tenants' associations. There is some evidence to suggest that those groups with a solid base in such activities are those with the greatest chance of survival. Thus one way to develop and sustain tenants' associations may be to provide them with a meeting place and the funds necessary to enable them to carry out such activities.

Why form?

Repairs, maintenance and rehabilitation matters were the reasons for formation most frequently cited by tenants' associations in our survey. Few (20 per cent) did not work on these issues currently. The popular view is that tenants' associations were formed in response to a housing problem. However, a wish to carry out a social and welfare role was mentioned by one in five tenants' associations and two-thirds included social and welfare activities among their work, ranging from dance classes and bingo to welfare rights advice and a library service for housebound tenants.

Those involved in tenants' associations also recognise their value as a channel of communication between individual tenants and the housing department or other bodies. Over 40 per cent of tenants' associations included contact with the housing department as part of their activities and it was also mentioned by some as a reason for formation.

> ***'[The TA is] the only forum we can communicate with the council, because individually you might go to the housing department or councillor, but the TA is recognised by the council and gives us the opportunity to bargain or discuss our problems.'***
> ***Council Tenant***

Less than a quarter of tenants' associations had a membership of over 300 members. Over two-fifths had no more than 100 members. As membership is sometimes automatic for all those living in the area, it is impossible to gauge the strength and vitality of a tenants' association from the size of its membership. One indicator is the ease with which it is able to recruit new members onto its management or executive committee. Three-quarters of all tenants' associations said that it was difficult to get new members to serve on their committees, and only two said that it was very easy.

POINTS TO COVER IN A TENANTS' ASSOCIATION CONSTITUTION, SUGGESTED BY TPAS (ENGLAND):

- Name of organisation
- Aims of organisation
- Membership – who can join
- Membership fee/subscription
- The committee – number, duties, how elected, frequency of meetings
- Annual general meetings – when and how will they be held, how will members be informed of them
- Other general meetings – when and how will they be held, how will members be informed of them
- Quorum for AGM and other meetings
- Changes to constitution – who can do it and how
- Dissolution – how can it be done and what will happen to the organisation's funds and possessions
- Standing orders – rules to be followed at meetings

TPAS 1989

Relationships with landlords

Tenants' associations adopt different attitudes towards the housing authority or association. Some groups are extremely suspicious and distrustful of the landlord and consequently employ a confrontational approach. In other cases, a close relationship exists between landlord and tenants, which some may think is at the cost of the group's independence. There is no right answer to the question of what is the best attitude or approach and tenants feel, sometimes acutely, the dilemma.

> ***'I wish I could make other people aware that housing associations are not always perfect. They're not con artists, but they are persuasive and I'd be frightened, if I joined the committee, of taking the association's side and not that of the tenants.'***
>
> ***Member of a Tenants' Association***
> ***(quoted in Platt et al, 1987)***

Where a tenants' association from its inception adopts a hostile attitude to the landlord it may alienate the support and sympathy of officers and councillors or management committee members. Most landlords expect tenants' groups to adopt a co-operative attitude, although they understand that where this fails to assist tenants in achieving their aims, they may become more strident and more militant. Most tenants' groups appear to become confrontational only after other approaches to their landlord have failed.

A confrontational tenants' association is often a sign that tenant participation has failed or that the tenants do not feel that participation is possible. It may, however, be caused by a lack of knowledge among the members of the constraints under which the landlord is working.

> ***'There is a tendency for the officers [or tenants' associations] to be kicking and trying to force the hand sometimes of elected members rather than getting in there and co-operating, and I think it is possibly a lack of understanding of the constraints which have been placed on local authorities at the moment. I suppose it's a thing of understanding the other side's problems, so I suppose in a way it's education. If they knew more then I think their attitude would be different. Quite often they can make demands which are impossible.'***
>
> ***Councillor***

It may take a long time and hard work by officers and councillors or committee members to change the attitudes of a hostile association and develop a good relationship with it.

The majority of tenants, whether or not they are actively involved in a tenants' association, see them as a useful and effective means of communication with the landlord. In the tenants' survey, less than one in ten tenants agreed with the view that: 'Elected councillors are the only people who should make decisions about council housing and tenants' associations should not get involved.' Most tenants wanted their landlord to give them more information and to involve them more in decisions about their housing. They thought that tenants' associations had a role to play in solving individual and collective housing problems, and in creating community spirit.

The skills that tenants need in order to participate depend on what process is involved and what methods are used. Members of tenants' groups often have useful skills already. For example, some tenants' association members have previous experience of trade union work and are able to bring valuable negotiating and bargaining abilities to the process of tenant participation. Members of tenants' groups may need to learn practical skills such as newsletter production, book-keeping, or how to chair a meeting or negotiate with the landlord. When a tenant plays a particular role within a tenant participation scheme, they may need role training. They may also lack expertise in some specialist area of housing, such as finance or law. There is a very low level of formal training provided by landlords: only two councils, both in Scotland, and one housing association, said that they provided training for tenants.

> ***'I think on the whole they [tenants' associations] have the skills . . . I have actually been pleasantly surprised by the way in which many tenants' groups can argue a case and present information. Whether they have the knowledge at this stage is another matter.'***
>
> ***Assistant Director of Housing***

Where a tenants' group lacks certain skills, it is not always necessary or appropriate for the landlord to provide training directly. Groups such as the local tenants' federation, TPAS or the local Workers Education Association, may be better placed to provide this. Alternatively, the tenants' group may want to 'buy in' the skill required, for example, from a Law Centre or an independent environmental health officer. Tenants' associations often do not call training by that name. It may take time and tact to find out what skills they lack, what training they would like, and how they want it to be provided.

Tenants' groups, like housing officers, councillors and members of management committees, have not been immune to charges of racism and sexism. If the landlord organisation does not have policies which it practises on these issues, tenants' groups will take a dim view of being exhorted to oppose racism or sexism themselves. If a tenants' association is non-racist and non-sexist, it has a strong base because it has a wider membership, greater reserves of experience and expertise to call upon, and a more united community. To achieve this, tenants' associations may need sensitive advice, plenty of encouragement, and resources from the landlord.

Resources

The resources that tenants' associations have available to them vary widely. In the survey most had access to a meeting room and a typewriter, but less than one in four had access to office supplies or premises, training or transport facilities, and less than two in five had access to expert advice. Those with access to independent expert advice, excluding council officers, are probably even fewer. Local authorities and housing associations can provide resources such as these directly or indirectly, but there is little evidence that many do so at present.

SOURCES OF INDEPENDENT ADVICE FOR TENANTS' ASSOCIATIONS

Tenants' federation
Tenant Participation Advisory Service
Law Centre
Citizens Advice Bureau
Community worker
Community Projects Foundation
Shelter
Local and national voluntary organisations

The revenue available to tenants' associations also varies considerably. Nearly one-third of those that gave financial details had an income below £50 a year. Membership fees and grants from the local authority were the most common sources of income. The wealthiest associations derived their main income from the local authority, the Manpower Services Commission (as it then was) and fees from licensed bars.

One in ten tenants' associations had to use members' flats or houses to hold their meetings, others used pubs. Although two-thirds were satisfied with the premises they used for meetings, some had complaints about the small size, state of repair, or distance from estate of the meeting places that they used. The cost of hire can also be a problem for a tenants' association trying to find a meeting place.

Without adequate funding, tenants' associations are obliged to rely on goodwill and informal networks in order to gain access to the resources they need. Their existence is one of hand-to-mouth survival. In such a condition of insecurity, they may find it difficult to meet the demands that arrangements for tenant participation inevitably place upon them.

Tenants

Individual tenants may participate in housing management in a number of different ways, of which three are most common:

- as individuals acting on their own behalf
- as representatives of tenants' associations or other voluntary organisations

- as representatives of tenants in an area or street or block, or in a more general sense as a representative of tenants' interests.

Each type of role poses some problems for tenants and landlords, and the differences between the roles are not always clear.

Tenants acting on their own behalf

Individual tenants may respond to an approach from the landlord or may initiate contact. In the latter case there is no clear distinction between tenants trying to participate in the management of their housing, and tenants wishing to make a complaint, report a repair or apply for a transfer, for example. The response the landlord makes to such routine approaches by tenants is important in determining the perception the tenant has of the landlord's attitude both to the housing service and to participation.

Where a landlord initiates contact, individual tenants may be informed or consulted by letter, or by more direct methods such as visits to tenants' homes inviting them to have a say or choose from a range of options. Such approaches are generally welcomed. Housing officers, however, report disappointing responses to consultation by individual letters, and uncertainty about how to interpret the results. Tenants can find it difficult to distinguish between letters which inform them and those which consult them, and may be sceptical about whether tenants' opinions would carry any weight. In addition, some tenants may be hesitant to make criticisms, or may prefer to leave the job of responding to others more involved, more extrovert or more knowledgeable. This emphasises the value of consulting tenants through tenants' associations and other voluntary organisations which bring tenants together.

Where groups do not exist landlords can play a role in assisting tenants to form them, but should not be put off as easily as the housing association reported in *Heard or Ignored.*

> ***'We sent round a circular about forming a tenant association, only about fifteen of the eighty tenants were interested and we didn't feel it was viable. The ones who wanted to join were the most fractious.'***
>
> *Committee Member*
> *(quoted in Platt et al, 1987)*

Many successful tenants' associations had even smaller beginnings, and were in time, able to direct the 'fractiousness' to constructive ends.

Tenants as representatives of groups

Tenants who participate in housing on behalf of a tenants' association or other voluntary group can face a variety of difficulties (discussed earlier in this chapter), relating to the resource and training needs of tenants' associations. Tenants can suffer isolation and uncertainty about how to play their role, and may have to acquire quickly a new range of skills and knowledge. The pressures, and lack of time and resources, can make it difficult for tenants to keep in touch with the group they purport to represent. Landlords should not place such burdens on tenants' representatives without providing support to enable them to carry out their responsibilities effectively.

Tenants representing tenants' interests

Tenants can act as representatives of tenants' interests without necessarily belonging to a tenants' group. Two common ways this occurs are through election at a public meeting, or at the invitation of the landlord, usually after the tenant has shown some interest in management issues. Playing this role poses difficulties and uncertainties.

> ***'There is no clear definition of our role. We are not elected by any tenant body or delegated in any way, so we are there as individuals, but I behaved as if I was speaking for other tenants.'***
>
> ***Tenant, Former Member of Management Committee (quoted in Platt et al, 1987)***

The difficulty of being seen to be accountable to other tenants is partly overcome in some housing associations and authorities by annual public meetings to elect representatives and report on the previous year's work. In such circumstances some landlords are not too concerned about representativeness.

References

Platt Steve, Piepe Rita and Smyth Judith (1987) *Heard or Ignored*, NFHA, London

TPAS Keynotes (1989) *Running a Tenants' Association*, TPAS, Salford

OUTCOMES AND ACHIEVEMENTS

6

CHAPTER

This chapter looks at what landlords have to gain from tenant participation. It examines five reasons for supporting tenant participation which are commonly put forward by housing managers, local councillors and housing association committee members.

The objectives of tenant participation

These reasons are, that tenant participation:

- helps community development
- leads to better housing management
- gives tenants more choice or more power
- leads to greater tenant satisfaction
- helps councillors and committee members to do their job.

Each of these is examined to see what they can mean in practice, how participation is meant to achieve them, and whether in fact it does. The discussion draws on evidence from interviews with housing managers, councillors and tenants in six local authority areas, from a household survey of tenants in these areas, and from *Heard or Ignored* (Platt et al, 1987).

The primary focus in this chapter is on the meaning and relevance of the objectives of landlords (housing managers, local councillors, and housing association committee members). However, the objectives of these various groups may differ, and may not correspond with those of tenants. These differences are important because they can profoundly influence whether any one party can achieve its objectives. For example, tenants may have as their primary objective the achievement of better housing conditions, but they are unlikely to achieve this if housing managers and committee members do not share the objective. The different processes of participation outlined in Chapter Four should be borne in mind and their applicability to the achievement of particular objectives has to be judged.

Helping community development?

The objective of helping community development through tenant participation can place emphasis on individual tenants, or on tenants collectively improving the quality of life in their area.

Tenant participation is said to improve the knowledge and skills of individual tenants and to contribute to changes in attitude towards their landlord and to society in general. Many housing managers, councillors, and committee members consider that tenants do not understand the constraints within which landlords have to work. They point to examples of tenants bringing forward good ideas which are impracticable for financial reasons. Tenant participation is seen as a way of passing on information to tenants so that they can understand why certain decisions have been taken and can formulate ideas and demands in the light of what is feasible. Also, it is envisaged that better knowledge of why decisions are made, and the development of personal relationships, will break down any animosities and make tenants better disposed towards their landlords.

In practice, there is evidence that experience of tenant participation can radically change the lives of some tenants. There are numerous examples of individuals who have developed knowledge and skills through running tenants' associations and through negotiation with their landlord. In some cases these new-found skills have been used to forge a political career; in others it has led to a new career in housing or other fields. Sometimes tenants are content to continue to use their skills in the service of their community. Whichever direction is taken the personal testimony of tenants bears witness to the strength of the impact which tenant participation can have.

> ***'By belonging to the tenants' association, I've seen a lot of things I never knew existed and it's made me much more aware of other people's problems. I think it's made me a better person. I feel now that I could go out and cope with a lot of things which I couldn't have done before. For instance, I never could have stood up and spoke in front of people. I would've been too nervous. And now I've joined the school governors and I never would have done that, because I wouldn't have thought I was good enough. It's made me feel better about myself and made me realise it's only everyday, ordinary people who do these things.'***
>
> ***Tenant***

However, there are two important constraints which should be recognised. First, this powerful impact is only achieved by intensive participation processes, such as dialogue and negotiation, or joint management or control. Providing information to tenants is unlikely *by itself* to achieve these powerful effects. Also, where tenants have little influence on their landlords they are likely to become discouraged and lose the motivation to develop their skills. Second, only a few tenant activists will benefit in this way to a large degree. Members of a management committee of tenants' association, for example, may gain new skills, but it is unlikely that other tenants would benefit to anywhere near the same extent.

There is evidence that the attitudes as well as the skills of participants may change with experience of tenant participation. The widespread perception of officers and councillors is that the attitudes of tenants, councillors, committee members and housing managers, do change as they come to realise that the other parties are 'only human' and may share the same motivation as themselves. Through close contact with landlord representatives, tenants can gain a better understanding of the motives and actions of these parties. Where participation occurs intensively, tenants and landlords appear able to agree to disagree on some issues while continuing a dialogue on other matters.

There is, however, little survey evidence that tenant participation on its own changes the attitudes of tenants towards their landlord. For example, in a recent study of the effectiveness of housing management (Centre for Housing Research, 1989) tenants were asked to indicate how they felt about their landlord in a number of respects such as whether it cared about tenants and whether it listened to them. The answers were found to be largely unrelated to the existence or extent of tenant participation, probably because only a few tenants will have had direct contact over a period of time with housing managers. Being seen at public meetings may help changes in attitudes, but more intensive contact as well as tangible achievements are needed if hostile attitudes are to be overcome.

In the survey of tenants in six local authorities, members of tenants' associations were more likely to have negative attitudes towards the council than non-members. It is difficult to explain such a result, but one factor may be that participation is often instituted in areas where there is considerable dissatisfaction with the service provided. This is often the spur for the formation of tenants' associations or for the involvement of tenants in attempts to change conditions on the estates.

Changes in tenants' attitudes, where they do occur, will depend on whether they consider the participation process to be a success. If housing managers are not perceived as acting from the best motives, do not succeed in building up trust, let the tenants down, or do not achieve practical results on the ground, it is unlikely that positive attitudes will result.

'Good participation is essentially participation which achieves results on the ground. It can result in attitudinal change, but it is practical results which bring about this change. Perhaps if they [tenants] were anti-local authority before and all that's happened is that they have had a chat about it with the housing manager, nothing has actually happened but they have had a nice time, had a cup of tea and a biscuit, then it won't fundamentally change their attitude, what would change it would be more trees on their estate a year after they had asked for them!'

Housing Officer

Tenant participation can also be seen as a means of assisting community development by fostering collective action by tenants to improve their quality of life. Tenant participation is said to lead to a stronger sense of community and to the encouragement of social networks of support and control. This should lead to collective action and to the reduction of problems, such as rent arrears, voids, vandalism and anti-social behaviour. It is argued that this results in tenants having a greater sense of commitment to their area and a feeling that they can influence conditions and the way that the area is perceived by outsiders and by the landlord. Collectively tenants can exert informal pressure on those who create problems for the landlord or for other tenants. This can be done by publicising problems and the impact they have on the area or by informing housing officers of problems as they arise. Alternatively, tenants can deal with problems directly through, for example, collective 'work-ins' to clean up the area, or bringing to the notice of individuals concerned the impact of their anti-social action.

There is considerable evidence that tenant participation can aid a sense of community and that tenants' associations are the key to achieving this. Two-thirds of tenants in the survey and 80 per cent of association members agreed with the statement that tenants' associations helped to create a community spirit. Some 20 per cent of tenants' associations mentioned the desire to organise social and welfare activities as a reason for formation and nine per cent mentioned the need to develop community spirit.

About half the tenants' associations said that they carried out social and welfare functions as part of their main activities and ten per cent listed the development of community spirit as one of their main activities. Apart from the direct social benefits this brings, such activities also build support for the association, enable it to keep in touch with its members, and give it a purpose if at any time there are no major housing issues to pursue. Associations which do not develop such activities seem to find it more difficult to survive than those which do. However, although some housing managers see a role for tenants' associations in dealing directly with issues such as anti-social behaviour which relate to individual tenants, this view is not shared by most tenants and by tenants' associations who view this as the landlord's responsibility.

Improving housing management?

Tenant participation is seen to result in better housing management through improving decisions by councillors, committee members and managers. It is argued that problems can be discovered at an early stage in their development and corrective action taken. The impact on tenants of changes in service provision can be assessed. Participation could thus provide housing managers with a subjective yardstick of their performance to supplement objective indicators (such as the void rate, or the level of rent arrears).

Tenants' associations, it is felt, can play a major role in this process by seeking out and collating the views of tenants and converting them into a collective view which decision-makers can take into account. This can improve the quality of the information reaching decision-makers as well as making their task easier. The result is held to be a better quality of housing service for the needs of local people.

It is very difficult to assess whether in fact tenant participation results in better management. This is mainly because it is difficult to assess the quality of housing management, but also because it is difficult to ascertain what would have happened if tenant participation had not taken place. In any situation tenant participation is only one of a number of factors which can influence performance.

Bearing these problems in mind, the evidence does not show a link between tenant participation and effective management performance. In the study of management performance in housing associations and local authorities in England (Centre for Housing Research, 1989) there was no sign that landlords who pursued policies of tenant participation were more effective managers than those who did not. However, this is not necessarily evidence that tenant participation is of no use in this regard, because many other factors may be at work. For example, metropolitan councils were more likely than other types of landlord to pursue tenant participation, but they had a less effective management service, largely because of their size when compared to other landlords.

The lesson to be learnt is not that tenant participation has no impact, rather it is that it is one factor amongst many which can influence performance, but it is unlikely on its own to turn a bad service into a good one. Nevertheless, the experience of officers, councillors and tenants is that it can be a valuable part of an attempt to improve performance. Great stress is placed by housing managers and councillors on the importance of channelling information about needs and the impact of services.

> *'I don't believe that housing departments and councillors know everything, and that the input by tenants in many cases is very important. It helps to shape decisions. It can also help to be economic in housing. I think it plays a vital part. I have always been one for consultation.'*
>
> *Councillor*

There was a widespread feeling among both housing managers and councillors that tenant participation had led to tenants being more committed to their homes and to the area, thus reducing management problems.

> *'They will take more interest in their homes and their surroundings, keep our properties in a better state of repair, they should be happier in their homes and their environment.'*
>
> *Housing Manager*

The general feeling is best summed up by one district housing manager with experience of tenant participation.

> *'You cannot manage properly unless the people whose homes we are managing are with us. They are their homes and they know a great deal more than we do. Even as officers we may think an issue is crystal clear and obvious, but it may be wrong because we haven't thought about all the angles. There are things that TAs can handle which we can't ... They can bring things to our attention which we may not be aware of. They can help us form our policies in such a way that they're going to be successful.'*
>
> *District Housing Manager*

The housing officers with experience of tenant participation accepted that it could take a lot of time and added to the pressures on them in the short term. Nevertheless, many considered it to be a rewarding experience which gave them a lot of job satisfaction both through actual achievements and through the process of working with tenants. There was also perceived to be a long-term pay off which made the extra effort worthwhile.

> *'It [tenant participation] probably makes the job more difficult, but it makes it more rewarding. The benefits of it are that in the end it makes your job easier. Hard work now for less work later if you like.'*
>
> *District Housing Manager*

There are limits, however, to how much work can be expected of tenants' associations. Some housing managers look to them to take work off their hands by dealing with questions of neighbour disputes or breaches of tenancy agreements. This strategy is counter-productive, because it creates tensions between tenants and the associations which are difficult to deal with and can lead to a loss of confidence in the association or even its demise. This can happen in particular where an association is formed to deal with a particular problem, but once this is resolved, the association can have problems adjusting to a new role.

> *'Once they [the tenants] get the [new/modernised] houses they find the tenants' association a bit of a thorn in their side sometimes, because the tenants' association are then turning the tables on them and they are going to see tenants saying you can't build that fence that high or tidy up your back garden or don't park your car on the front garden/verge and let oil spill all over the place and they just turn round and tell them where to get off and, of course, the tenants' association say if that's what they want I am just going to look after myself. They don't have the support afterwards.'*
>
> *District Housing Manager*

This highlights the importance of housing officers being sensitive to the pressures which tenants' associations can face and not expecting associations to manage the estate for them without the necessary authority.

Giving tenants more choice and power?

The objective of giving tenants more choice and more power sees tenant participation as an end in itself as well as a means to a particular end. It is based either on a moral, philosophical principle or on practical grounds. The principle is supported usually by reference either to a view about the value of participative democracy, or to a view about the importance of customers' rights.

The view that tenants, as customers of the housing service, are entitled to participate in its management is very widely held by housing managers. It has achieved particular prominence since the introduction of the 1988 Housing Act and the realisation that customers can opt to transfer to another landlord.

> *'I am a professional housing person and I have a quite deep-rooted desire to offer a good service, and the only way you can do this is to ... the only way the customer will think it is a good service is to give them what they want.'*
>
> *Housing Manager*

> *'We are acting on behalf of them. They are paying for the service, they elected us to do the job yes, but if we ignore their wishes it is at our own peril.'*
>
> *Chairperson of Housing*

The view that tenants have intrinsic democratic rights to participation is perhaps less widely held by housing managers. Nevertheless, many councillors from all parts of the political spectrum believe it to be consistent with their political philosophy. However, choice and power are not absolute concepts and there are considerable disagreements about how much choice and power are appropriate and over the spheres in which they can legitimately be exercised.

There are many examples where tenant participation has expanded the choice which tenants can exercise. For example, in some renewal schemes tenants collectively are given the opportunity to decide jointly with technical staff what work will be carried out (IoH/RIBA, 1988). Obviously there are financial and technical constraints on the choices which can be made.

Choice can be offered in different ways. Tenants can be constrained in their choice by a limited range of options, a lack of knowledge of the implications of particular courses of action, or of how to challenge the judgements of housing managers.

> *'In my previous authority we had an open-ended approach where we came with a blank piece of paper and said, right we're going to do your housing up, what do you want? What we tend to do in my present authority is say we're going to do up your houses, what do you want: A, B or C?'*
>
> *District Housing Manager*

Tenant participation does give tenants collectively the power to influence the management of their houses, but the degree of power will differ considerably for the same reasons which can influence the degree of choice. However, it is worth remembering that tenants' groups have little power over the management of their houses and are dependent on the landlord to cede power to them. Their powerlessness can be illustrated by the ability of landlords to summarily suspend tenant participation when it suits them. There are many examples of a change of political control in a local authority resulting in the cessation of tenant participation. Therefore, it is important for landlords to realise that the amount of power which can be exercised by tenants depends crucially on decisions made by the landlord and on the participation processes which they are willing to institute.

Increasing tenant satisfaction?

The objective of trying to achieve more satisfied tenants through tenant participation is pursued currently for two major reasons. First, tenant satisfaction is one of the prime social objectives of council and housing association housing. Tenant participation is said to assist in identifying problems, in providing feedback on services and in ensuring friendly and constructive relations between tenants and landlord. Fewer problems are, therefore, likely to emerge and housing managers can devote more time to strategic issues and to the development of services.

Secondly, satisfied council tenants are more likely to stay with their present landlord. Tenant participation is seen to assist councils who wish to hold on to their tenants and housing stock after the 1988 housing legislation. Tenant participation is felt to provide councils with the insights they require to ensure tenants are sufficiently satisfied with the service not to seek or be attracted to alternative landlords.

In practice, it is difficult to show that by itself tenant participation leads to satisfied tenants. In the review of housing management in England (Centre for Housing Research, 1989) it was evident that tenant satisfaction was more strongly related to the quality of service provided to tenants than to the degree of tenant involvement. Tenant participation was only one of many factors which appeared to influence tenant satisfaction. Even in areas of relatively well developed tenant participation there was a substantial demand from tenants for more. Indeed the demand for further participation was stronger in those areas where it already existed than where it did not exist. In other words instituting limited tenant particpation may raise expectations which are not fulfilled and, therefore, can lead to more dissatisfaction. Tenant participation should be seen as one constituent of effective housing management and not as a panacea.

Tenant satisfaction also depends on the outcome of tenant participation. Tenants have positive or negative views of participation processes and on whether they have had what they consider to be an appropriate say. However, tenants mostly see tenant participation as a means to an end rather than as an end in itself. Therefore, they are likely to judge participation by whether it achieves the desired results.

> ***'I feel that if tenants are consulted they are much happier about the local housing department and the council. If they are not consulted they feel out of it and bitter. That can cause problems.'***
>
> ***Councillor***

Housing managers and councillors see tenant participation as a key tool in making tenants more satisfied both as an end in itself and as a means of encouraging tenants to remain with them.

> *'In the current climate tenant participation is crucial. With Tenants' Choice it is crucial that they get the idea that the authority is trying to help them.'*
>
> *Councillor*

> *'The ultimate objective is to make sure they stay with us.'*
>
> *Housing Manager*

The general view was that tenant participation did help to raise tenant satisfaction, but its impact on the propensity of tenants to stay with their landlord was open to conjecture.

Helping committee members play their part?

Most councillors of all political persuasions, and many housing association committee members believe that tenant participation helps them to carry out their role more effectively. It is said to do this in a number of ways.

First, it creates a channel of communication between members and tenants, making it easier for members to gauge the views of tenants and assess the impact of decisions upon them. Tenants' associations can be particularly useful in passing on a collective view. Secondly, participation can act as an early warning system for problems or defects in service which could damage a councillor's or committee member's support amongst tenants, or dent the caring image of the landlord. Thirdly, tenant participation can create a direct channel between tenants and housing managers which means that councillors and committee members are less likely to be asked to deal with individual tenants' complaints unless the problem cannot be dealt with at an early stage. The influence of councillors and committee members may then be useful in resolving the matter. In addition, they are able to spend more time on strategic issues. Fourthly, participation acts as a means of passing information to tenants. This can be useful in communicating to tenants the constraints within which landlords have to work. It can also serve to publicise decisions made and the work done by members. And finally, the existence of a tenants' association can give councillors and committee members an alternative source of information to that provided by officers. This can help them to make up their minds on issues and aid them to exercise control in policy making.

These views about the assistance tenant participation provides were broadly shared by the councillors interviewed, although there were significant differences in the extent and scope of tenant participation considered desirable.

The only negative views voiced concerned the possible threat which tenant activists could pose if they were to challenge councillors by standing for election themselves. However, the general consensus was that this was most likely to happen if councillors ignored existing tenants' groups and, therefore, any good councillor would become actively involved and respond to the needs of the tenants' association.

> *'If you find tenant participation threatening then you are not a good councillor, because if you are afraid of opposition then you can't be doing your job right. But if you antagonise them [tenants' groups] and don't meet with them then they're going to bring someone forward to challenge you eventually, because you haven't listened to what they're saying. You haven't carried the public with you.'*
>
> *Chairperson of Housing*

On balance almost all councillors felt that the advantages of tenants' associations and tenant participation outweighed any possible disadvantages.

> *'The benefit is to the council because then they get the feeling of the people. If there is something going wrong, rather than it being underlying, then it would come out and you can do something about it.'*
>
> *Chairperson of Housing Committee*

However, councillors were concerned with the tactics of tenants' associations which were considered to be crucial in aiding or hindering them in their job. For example, it was considered to be unhelpful to use aggressive campaigning methods, such as organising marches, or using the press, before all other forms of action had been exhausted. In other words associations were expected to engage in a constructive dialogue with the councillor. If this broke down and tenants had not achieved their objectives they were considered to have the right to use any means at their disposal and the councillor would have to take the consequences. However, recourse to methods such as using the press, and mass lobby at an earlier stage was seen to make a councillor's job more difficult.

> *'It [such public aggressive tactics] just might make people move a bit further, but there is always another side to the coin. Sometimes they will do that when it doesn't help at all and the problem with that is that it creates a kind of distrust and it doesn't help for anything which happens in the future.'*
>
> *Councillor*

The views of councillors seem to be broadly shared by housing association committee members, who also remain sceptical about particular forms of participation.

'Just over half the committee members were in favour of having tenants on the committee. However, one-third were totally opposed to it.'

(Platt et al, 1987)

The contribution to good tenant/landlord relations that tenants' associations can make was described by committe members of one association.

'"They [tenants' associations] get financial support and premises. Less than half are functioning, but are valuable nonetheless – it keeps the door open. None have totally lapsed as far as I know."... Another committee member said "We have had this kind of involvement for at least ten years. It has grown from small beginnings and over a hundred representatives turn up to the four joint meetings we hold each year."'

(Platt et al, 1987)

Conclusion

Tenant participation is not a panacea, but the experience of officers, committee members, councillors, and tenants is that it is a valuable tool to be used in achieving the objectives outlined here. The crudity of the research tools available and the difficulty of isolating tenant participation from other causal factors mean that it is futile to wait for conclusive proof that tenant participation is effective. Perhaps the value of the evidence gained so far is to show that other factors such as the provision of a good service are important.

Most of those with experience of tenant participation consider it to be a rewarding process which, although needing considerable time and effort in the short term, can bring substantial rewards. There are many examples where tenant participation for various reasons has not lived up to expectations, but many more cases where it has been successful. The following comments by a housing officer give a flavour of what can be achieved.

'I worked for x where we had a good staff/tenant ratio and you had the time to do proper tenant consultation and proper tenant consultation is quite rewarding really. We had an open-ended approach where we came in with a blank piece of paper and said right we're going to do your housing up, what do you want, what we tend to do here is we're going to do your houses up, what do you want: A, B or C? Although we do consult we don't really consult as much as we could do.

I had a project in x where we were doing up a really rundown estate. We worked there, we got PEP money to set up a house on the estate which became an office. We used a lot of graphics, a very high-tech approach. We put a lot of legwork in, a lot of time outside normal working hours. We sat down and thought about it first, we brought other departments in on it. We put on a good show, you known tea and coffee for the tenants not just sitting them down in hard wooden chairs and saying right here's what you've got, choose A or B. We discussed it with them and said what do you think have been the problems on the estate and how as professional people do you think we . . . you can change that given that we have got x amount of money. And all we did then was sit back and say well you can't have that because . . . but if you could have it then give them it. At the end of the day when it's all finished they all came back and said great, and those who did come back and say you know I didn't want this, or this hasn't worked, to some extent we can point the finger at them then and say well we gave you carte blanche and this is what you wanted. Of course, in the end, we had an idea of what we wanted and to some extent we herded them a bit like sheepdogs towards what we wanted to do. Again dealing with tenants who had little idea of how much things cost obviously we were there to say that's well over the top, we haven't got that much money, but how about this? That was very rewarding and did go a long way towards achieving tenants' satisfaction.

We did figures before and after and there was a high level of rent arrears, there was a high level of voids and there was a high level of transfer requests, and then we did a survey afterwards, not straight afterwards, because that would have given a bit of a false impression, so we did the survey a year later when it was finished. We went back and it has even affected the level of rent arrears which was surprising to us. People were paying their rent whereas people before weren't, nobody wanted to move and there was less complaint.'

Housing Officer

References

Centre for Housing Research (1989) *The Nature and Effectiveness of Housing Management in England*, DoE, HMSO, London

Platt Steve, Piepe Rita and Smyth Judith. (1987) *Heard or Ignored*, NFHA, London

IoH/RIBA (1988) *Tenant Participation in Housing Design*, IoH/RIBA, London

CHAPTER 7

STANDARDS AND PERFORMANCE

Standards and targets for tenant participation are not well developed. The complex and sometimes controversial nature of participation makes it a difficult aspect of housing management to evaluate. This chapter looks at possible approaches to setting appropriate targets and standards for tenant participation.

Setting standards and targets

How should performance be measured when a housing authority or association is consulting tenants over a modernisation project, for example? Should it be judged by the turnout at a public meeting, or by whether tenants were well-informed about the proposals, or by whether their views were listened to, or by the degree of choice over the modernisation offered to tenants, or by the views of tenants about the participation process? Very often housing officers choose one readily available target, such as high attendance at a public meeting, and judge all their participation efforts against a standard which may be set unrealistically high.

To provide a fuller evaluation of participation requires a more complex set of standards and targets which take account of the complexity of participation and the objectives of the authority or association in the first place. Standards and targets can be set only with reference to more specific methods and processes of participation and with reference to the objectives of the landlord and tenants. Some reference to tenants' views is an essential part of evaluating performance.

Broadly there are two types of standard or target that can be set: **objective** and **subjective** measures; and each can be set or examined in absolute terms, or by reference to the relative position of one landlord as against another.

An objective standard for participation may be to assist the formation of a tenants' group on all the estates owned by a regional housing association. If, say, only six groups exist and there are twelve estates, an appropriate target may be to assist tenants in the remaining six estates to form groups. Relative to another similar housing association with two groups in existence, the first association may feel that it is performing well. But if its tenants do not wish to form more groups or think that those which exist do not achieve anything, then these subjective views of the tenants may provide a gloomier picture of the association's performance.

Each landlord must devise its own set of standards and monitoring procedures and should try to do so in association with tenants' representatives. This chapter is intended to assist by highlighting the issues to be addressed, and by providing some examples of targets and ways of monitoring performance.

Associations will have to decide on targets which are most appropriate to their own aims and policies. The following are examples of general targets which can be set within the area of tenant involvement and access to services. When possible we also recommend some specific targets, the levels of performance which we believe associations may wish to adopt. Associations may have very good reasons for choosing higher or lower targets. The main point is to set some targets and endeavour to achieve them.

NFHA, 1987

Methods

Quality and quantity both need to be considered in setting standards and targets for different methods of participation. For example, quantitative targets may be set for the production of written communications to tenants, but these would not take account of the value to tenants of the information, nor of the extent to which it accurately conveyed the message that the landlord wished to get over. So quality needs to be considered as well as quantity. Examples of targets and standards are shown in the box on page 102.

Targets that relate to quantity can be a useful spur to action, and can be relatively easily monitored. Targets could be adopted for all the forms of written communication discussed in Chapter Three – adverts, posters and notices; leaflets; handbooks and packs; newsletters; letters to individuals and groups. Equally targets could be set for achieving forms of face to face contact, from tenant representation on committees to occasional meetings between tenants and their landlord's representatives. However, it should not be assumed that more means better. For example, regular meetings between tenants and landlord should be held at intervals which allow time for investigations between meetings, so monthly may be preferable to weekly meetings. The optimal frequency will depend, amongst other things, on the process of participation the meetings are intended to further (see Chapter Four and below).

Standards or targets that relate to quality are perhaps more difficult to devise and monitor. The quality of written communication could be judged against 'objective' standards set, for example, by the Plain English Campaign, and also according to the subjective evaluation of tenants. Tenants' views can be collected through surveys, or during face to face contact on substantive housing issues. Standards for face to face contact could be incorporated in a code of practice covering issues such as access to the agenda, neutrality of chairing, resources for tenant participation for example child care provision, and convenience of meeting venues and times. Monitoring of whether such standards are achieved can be done through observation and by seeking the views of the participants. Specialist community development staff can play a role here, perhaps in providing training for staff who are unskilled in conducting discussions with tenants.

METHODS OF PARTICIPATION: EXAMPLES OF STANDARDS AND TARGETS

Method: written communication	■ **information pack is revised at least every two years** ■ **information is available in minority languages** ■ **newsletter is produced monthly**
Method: face to face contact	■ **tenants have access to area managers** ■ **tenants' representatives meet monthly with tenant liaison officer** ■ **seminar takes place on policy reviews**

As well as considering targets for communication and contact, landlords should consider the substantive issues on which they are willing to participate. As Chapter Three demonstrates, many councils and housing associations have in practice restricted participation to a small number of the wide range of potential issues on which tenants may wish to participate. It is essential to be explicit about which issues are open for debate or information provision and which are not. Some issues, such as equal opportunities policies, may be non-negotiable. Having set the agenda and the targets, monitoring should attempt to ensure that the issues specified have been the subject of participation. For example, a progress report on the nature and outcome of participation could be a standard item on each committee agenda. Consideration should also be given to extending or reducing the range of issues in the light of experience.

Landlords should also consider the geographical levels at which particular issues will be the subject of participation. Allocation policies, for example, may be considered an appropriate topic for consultation at neighbourhood, area/district, and authority/association wide levels, but not at the individual level. Targets could be devised for extending the levels at which different issues are the subject of communication or face to face contact.

A further set of standards or targets relate to tenants' associations. Here landlords might set targets for assisting the formation of groups, for providing resources, training and advice, and for the conduct of relations with groups. Standards can be set by means of a code of practice which states the landlord's policy or target for replying to queries, attending meetings, recognising tenants' associations, and for providing resources such as crèches.

FOSTERING TENANTS' ASSOCIATIONS: STANDARDS AND TARGETS

POLICY	Examples of standards or targets
Provision of resources	■ starting grants of £100 ■ negotiate levy on tenants' rents to support tenants' movement ■ three year programme for development of meeting places in all estates
Fostering good relationships	■ consultation with tenants' associations at quarterly meetings with director and chairperson ■ designation of liaison officer in each area office
Fostering new groups	■ tenant participation officer to approach tenants in areas undergoing modernisation ■ training to be provided for new office-bearers

PROCESSES OF PARTICIPATION: EXAMPLES OF STANDARDS AND TARGETS

PROCESSES	Examples of standards and targets
Providing information to tenants	■ tenants know what they are supposed to know ■ follow plain English and ethnic minority language guidelines ■ 75 per cent say received handbook
Seeking information from tenants	■ tenants feel opinions valued
Listening	■ chairpersons trained to facilitate participation by tenants at joint meetings ■ tenants feel landlord listens
Consultation	■ setting timetable to allow consideration of views ■ providing tenants' groups with six weeks to respond to housing investment plan
Dialogue	■ papers and minutes of committee meetings circulated to tenants' representatives ■ officers/tenants feel other is responding
Joint management	■ a joint management committee is established in all difficult-to-let estates ■ one new joint committee is established each year ■ tenants' representatives are satisfied that joint committee is working
Choice	■ choice of heating system offered in modernisation
Control	■ tenants in management co-ops satisfied ■ staffing of promotions unit increased from one to two ■ at least one new management co-op established each year

Processes Participation involves one or more processes. Standards and targets should, therefore, relate to whether and how the processes of participation take place. Issues of quantity and quality arise. First, standards should provide the means to assess whether a particular process has actually taken place: were the views of tenants considered seriously? Was choice offered? Was decision making shared? Targets can also be adopted for extending the processes on offer for example from consultation to dialogue (see box). Authorities and associations will, however, want to go beyond clarifying which processes are engaged in, to examining the nature of the participation involved. Were tenants satisfied that their views were considered? Was the dialogue conducted in a fair and equitable manner? Were the choices meaningful to tenants? The quality of the processes can be judged by the observations of disinterested outsiders and by the participants themselves. An important criterion should be the views of the tenants themselves about the nature and quality of the choice or process of participation they were involved in.

The participants

Tenant participation should be added to the aspects of housing management considered in staff appraisal and staff development programmes. Senior and more junior staff should together agree on the targets to be set for specific tasks, and on any continuing standards or targets that should influence particular jobs. The targets set for individual staff members can be examined and reviewed at routine appraisal or development meetings. Examples of the standards that might be set for the work of a housing assistant and housing manager/chief housing officer are provided in the box on page 106.

Specific designated members of staff should be held responsible for achieving the standards adopted by authorities and associations. It is only occasionally that specialist tenant liaison or community development staff will be the appropriate people to ensure targets are met. If, for example, a housing association has a policy of meeting monthly with tenants' representatives on each estate, then it may be area officers who are held responsible for carrying this out. Specialist staff may be held responsible for ensuring that training and advice are provided.

Participation does not just involve housing staff as services to tenants may be provided on behalf of the landlord by other departments, agencies or private contractors. In these circumstances the landlord is a client of these departments or agencies and should insist that the latter's staff and services conform to certain standards of conduct. Similarly, councillors and management committee members may not feel bound by the same targets or standards that affect housing staff. If efforts to adopt consistent standards fail, there is a limit to what housing professionals can do.

STANDARDS FOR STAFF

Housing Assistant

- **assist tenants' groups with information and advice on request**
- **organise dialogue between tenants' representatives and the local repairs team**
- **meet tenants' association committee/office bearers monthly**
- **organise distribution of written information to new tenants**

Housing Manager/Chief Housing Officer

- **monitor implementation of participation policy**
- **consult tenants' groups annually about proposed rents rise**
- **meet tenants' federation representatives monthly**
- **foster new tenants' groups and administer 'starter' grants scheme**
- **review annual contents of tenants' information leaflets/pack**
- **ensure training made available for staff and tenants**

Measuring outcomes and achievements

Ultimately tenants and landlords will want to know whether the objectives for tenant participation have been achieved.

*community development

This objective does not lend itself easily to monitoring or evaluation. Community development may be furthered by activities other than tenant participation, making it difficult to measure the effect of tenant participation itself. In addition, measuring whether community development has taken place is not easy, and evaluation has to take account of the relative position within a community before and after attempts at tenant participation.

Targets commonly set include

- the creation or further development of tenants' groups
- the establishment of a structure or mechanism within which tenants may exercise influence
- the achievement of changes or improvements to the housing conditions or services within an area
- the articulation of demands or wishes by tenants in a manner which is seen as constructive by the landlord.

*better housing management

This objective implies tenant participation will provide valuable information to decision makers and ultimately lead to more satisfied tenants.

Evaluating whether better housing management has resulted therefore involves judgements about the quantity and quality of information provided by tenants. These are not easy judgements to make and it is difficult to extricate the impact of participation from other factors which influence tenant satisfaction.

The information provided by tenant participation may be a consequence of the resources devoted to its collection. Landlords need to consider the cost effectiveness of their efforts, not just the actual cost. Kay, Legg and Foot (undated) report several examples of relatively expensive and unproductive attempts to consult tenants by use of individual letters. Similar sums of money spent, for example, on organising small discussion meetings or sample surveys might have elicited more systematic or detailed information on tenants' views. Where heavy reliance is placed on tenants' associations to transmit the views of tenants, landlords should consider targets for resourcing tenants' groups and for collecting information by other means.

*more choice or power to tenants

This objective will be achieved in tangible ways such as providing choice over individual improvements, or involvement in collective decision making; and in intangible ways such as when tenants feel they have influenced outcomes but could not be certain what the outcomes would have been without their involvement.

The achievement of this objective can be evaluated by a combination of objective and subjective measures. Targets can be set, for example, in relation to the degree of choice offered to individual tenants, and the extent to which tenants' representatives are involved in dialogue and decision making. Subjective measures involve tenants' and landlord's judgements about the extent to which choice or power is exercised.

*more satisfied tenants

This objective will not necessarily be achieved by the use of tenant participation and there is evidence that its achievement is more likely to be a consequence of housing management services such as repairs. However, tenant participation may play a crucial role in helping to identify the problematic areas of the housing service and ways of dealing with them, and this is linked with the objective of achieving better housing management. Landlords should also consider whether tenants are satisfied with the arrangements for participation. A variety of methods can be used to assess this, including surveys, regular contact between managers and tenants and special working parties.

*helping councillors and committee members

This objective is achieved if councillors or committee members *feel* that tenant participation is helpful to them. The information provided by tenants can give insights into how the services or policies are affecting them. Officers and tenants may not feel it is the most important objective, but its achievement may help to facilitate other objectives.

Monitoring

If targets and standards are set, then housing managers and others will wish to know whether they are being met or achieved. Monitoring and evaluation are, therefore, required. Some monitoring is easily carried out – files and records should provide information on, for example, the number of tenants' groups, frequency of meetings and attendance rates. Most of the objective targets should be relatively easily monitored through adjustments to routine administrative recording systems. But many of the subjective targets require a special effort to be made to collect information, particularly from tenants. Some useful evaluation could be undertaken by asking tenants' representatives who are in contact with the landlord to provide views on their specific experiences of participation. Other opportunities could be taken to seek the views of tenants who are frequently in contact with housing managers. Finally, almost any systematic survey of tenants being undertaken, for example, as part of a modernisation project, could include some questions on tenants' views of the participation efforts of the landlord.

Housing authorities and associations cannot monitor or assess constantly their attainment of the multiplicity of standards that might be set for different aspects of participation. They should, however, guard against over-simplistic evaluations and develop a number of key targets with appropriate monitoring or evaluation arrangements. Any existing procedures for evaluating performance in housing management more generally, such as customer surveys, should of course be extended to encompass participation if they do not already do so. No definitive list of key targets has been recommended. Authorities and associations should select their own on the basis of the available resources and their most pressing objectives.

References

Kay Adah, Legg Charles and Foot Jane (undated) *The 1980 Tenants Rights in Practice*, The City University, London

National Federation of Housing Associations (1987) *Standards for Housing Management*, NFHA, London

RESEARCH METHOD

This report was the product of a three year research project funded by the Joseph Rowntree Memorial Trust, which built on the results of a survey of local authorities and housing associations in England, carried out by the Centre for Housing Research on behalf of the Department of the Environment.

APPENDIX

The following research methods were used:

- National survey of local authorities carried out over 1986–1987, which elicited responses from 282 councils in England, Scotland and Wales. This represents a response rate of sixty-two per cent which did not appear to be skewed in terms of size of authority.
- Survey of housing associations in England with a total stock of 200 or more properties, including special needs housing, but whose main activity is the provision of general needs housing. Seventy-seven associations responded. This represents a response rate of thirty-nine per cent.
- Case studies of six local authorities in Britain which were selected to reflect the variety of responses which were encountered in the national survey of local authorities.

Within these case studies, the following research methods were used:

- In-depth semi-structured interviews with approximately thirty-five council officers, and a similar number of active tenants' association members and councillors.
- Survey of all known tenants' associations, to which 142 responded, carried out in Spring 1988.

- Survey of 984 tenants in areas selected within the case studies to represent varying degrees of tenant activity, completed in Winter 1988.
- Examination of documentary evidence relating to tenant participation such as council minutes, newspaper articles and tenants' association newsletters.

Further reading

1. Andrews, L. (1979) *Tenants and Town Hall*, DoE, HMSO, London
2. Boaden N., Goldsmith M., Hampton W. and Stringer P. (1982) *Public Participation in Local Services*, Longman
3. Deakin N. and Wright A. (eds) (1989) *Consuming Public Services*, Routledge, London
4. Pateman C. (1970) *Participation and Democratic Theory*, Cambridge University Press, Cambridge
5. Richardson A. (1983) *Participation*, Routledge, London

All four Tenant Participation Advisory Services produce a range of publications aimed at landlords and tenants seeking to develop tenant participation. Publications lists are available from the addresses provided in the next section.

USEFUL CONTACTS

Association of Community
Technical Aid Centres (ACTAC)
64 Mount Pleasant
LIVERPOOL
L3 5SD
Tel: 051 708 7607

Centre for Public Services
1 Sidney Street
SHEFFIELD
S1 4EE
Tel: 0742 726683

Chartered Institute of Housing
Octavia House
Westwood Way
COVENTRY
CV4 8JP
Tel: 0203 694433

Chartered Institute of Housing
(Scotland)
6 Palmerston Place
EDINBURGH
EH12 5AA
Tel: 031 225 4544

Chartered Institute of Housing
(Wales)
4th Floor
Dominions House North
Queen Street
CARDIFF
CF1 4AR
Tel: 0222 397402

Community Architecture
Resource Centre
Royal Institute of British
Architects
66 Portland Place
LONDON
W1N 4AD
Tel: 071 580 5533

Community Development
Foundation
60 Highbury Grove
LONDON
N5 2AG
Tel: 071 226 5375

Community Rights Project
9 Cynthia Street
LONDON
N1 9JF
Tel: 071 713 7130

Department of the
Environment
2 Marsham Street
LONDON
SW1P 3EB
Tel: 071 276 3000

Federation of Black Housing
Organisations
374 Gray's Inn Road
LONDON
WC1X 8BB
Tel: 071 837 8288

Federation of Independent
Advice Centres
13 Stockwell Road
LONDON
SW9 9AU
Tel: 071 274 1839

Housing Centre Trust
20 Vestry Street
LONDON
N1 7RE
Tel: 071 253 6103

Law Centres Federation
18-19 Warrent Street
LONDON
W1P 5DB
Tel: 071 387 8570

National Association for the
Care and Resettlement of
Offenders
(NACRO)
169 Clapham Road
LONDON
SW9 OPU
Tel: 071 582 6500

National Association of
Citizens Advice Bureaux
(NACAB)
115-123 Pentonville Road
LONDON
N1 9LZ
Tel: 071 833 2181

National Consumer Council
20 Grosvenor Gardens
LONDON
SW1W 0DH
Tel: 071 730 3469

National Federation of
Housing Associations
175 Gray's Inn Road
LONDON
WC1X 8UP
Tel: 071 278 6571

National Tenants and Residents
Federation (NTRF)
c/o Kirklees Federation
41/42 Estate Buildings
Railway Street
HUDDERSFIELD
HD1 1JY
Tel: 0484 434943

National Tenants Organisation
c/o Voluntary Action Centre
12 School Road
MIDDLESEX
TW3 1QN
Tel: 081 569 5823

National Tower Blocks Network
Canning Town Public Hall
105 Barking Road
LONDON
E16 4HQ
Tel: 071 473 2270

Neighbourhood Initiatives Foundation
The Poplars
Lightmoor
TELFORD
TF4 3QN
Tel: 0952 590777

Plain English Campaign
Outram House
Canal Street
Whaley Bridge
STOCKPORT
SK12 7LS
Tel: 0663 345541

Priority Estate Project
2 Albert Mews
Albert Road
LONDON
N4 3RD
Tel: 071 281 0438

Scottish Consumer Council
Royal Exchange House
100 Queen Street
GLASGOW
G1 3DN
Tel: 041 226 5261

Scottish Federation of Housing Associations
38 York Place
EDINBURGH
EH1 3HU
Tel: 031 556 5777

Shelter (England)
88 Old Street
LONDON
EC1V 9HU
Tel: 071 253 0202

Shelter (Scotland)
65 Cockburn Street
EDINBURGH
EH1 1BU
Tel: 031 226 6347

Shelter (Wales)
25 Walter Road
SWANSEA
West Glamorgan
SA1 5NN
Tel: 0792 469400

Tenant Information Service (TIS)
Unit 16
Meadow Mill
West Henderson Wyde
DUNDEE
DD1 5BY
Tel: 0382 25012

TPAS National and Northern Office
48 The Crescent
SALFORD
M5 4NW
Tel: 061 745 7903

TPAS East
1st floor
22 High Street
Histon
CAMBRIDGE
CB4 4JD
Tel: 0223 235148

TPAS London and South-East
130 Eversholt Street
LONDON
NW1 1DL
Tel: 071 383 2778

TPAS Midlands
Adderley House
St. Peters Urban Village
Bridge Road
Saltley
BIRMINGHAM
B8 3TE
Tel: 021 327 3115

TPAS South-West
8 The Hide Market
West Street
BRISTOL
BS2 0BH
Tel: 0272 414144

TPAS Scotland
20/24 St Andrew's Street
GLASGOW
G1 5PD
Tel: 041 552 3633

TPAS Wales
2nd Floor
Transport House
1 Cathedral Road
CARDIFF
CF1 9SD
Tel: 0222 237303

Welsh Consumer Council
Castle Buildings
Womanby Street
CARDIFF
CF1 2BN
Tel: 0222 396056

Welsh Federation of Housing Associations
Norbury House
Norbury Road
Fairwater
CARDIFF
CF5 3AS
Tel: 0222 555022